Miniature Schnauzer

2nd Edition

GET MORE!
Visit www.wiley.com/
go/min_schnauzer

Elaine Waldorf Gewirtz

Howell
Book House™

Copyright © 2006 by Wiley Publishing, Inc., Hoboken, New Jersey. All rights reserved.

Howell Book House
Published by Wiley Publishing, Inc., Hoboken, New Jersey

For general information on our other products and services or to obtain technical support please contact our Customer Care Department within the U.S. at (800) 762-2974, outside the U.S. at (317) 572-3993 or fax (317) 572-4002.

Wiley also publishes its books in a variety of electronic formats. Some content that appears in print may not be available in electronic books. For more information about Wiley products, please visit our web site at www.wiley.com.

Library of Congress Cataloging-in-Publication Data:
Gewirtz, Elaine Waldorf.
     Miniature schnauzer / Elaine Waldorf Gewirtz.—2nd ed.
          p. cm.—(Your happy healthy pet)
     ISBN-13: 978-0-471-74828-1 (cloth : alk. paper)
     ISBN-10: 0-471-74828-5 (cloth : alk. paper)
     1. Miniature schnauzer. I. Title. II. Series.
     SF429.M58G49 2006
     636.755—dc22

Printed in the United States of America

10 9 8 7 6 5 4 3 2 1

2nd Edition

Photo research by Marcella Durand
Book design by Melissa Auciello-Brogan
Cover design by Michael J. Freeland
Illustrations in chapter 9 by Shelley Norris and Karl Brandt
Book production by Wiley Publishing, Inc. Composition Services

About the Author

Elaine Waldorf Gewirtz is the author of or a contributor to *Pugs For Dummies, Your Yorkshire Terrier's Life, The Dog Sourcebook, Dogs: The Ultimate Care Guide,* and *Dogspeak.* She has also written numerous magazine articles about dogs. She is a multiple winner of the Dog Writers Association of America's Maxwell Award for Excellence, and the recipient of the ASPCA Special Writing Award.

A graduate of UCLA's Masters in Writing program, Elaine is a member of the Dog Writers Association of America, the American Society of Journalists and Authors, and the Independent Writers of Southern California. She has lived with Miniature Schnauzers and other breeds all her life. Elaine writes the Dalmatian breed column for the *AKC Gazette,* breeds and shows Dalmatians in obedience and conformation, and teaches all-breed conformation classes.

She shares her home in Westlake Village, California, with her husband, Steve. The couple has four grown children: Sameya, Sara and husband Ryan, Seth, and Beth-Jo.

About Howell Book House

Since 1961, Howell Book House has been America's premier publisher of pet books. We're dedicated to companion animals and the people who love them, and our books reflect that commitment. Our stable of authors—training experts, veterinarians, breeders, and other authorities—is second to none. And we've won more Maxwell Awards from the Dog Writers Association of America than any other publisher.

As we head toward the half-century mark, we're more committed than ever to providing new and innovative books, along with the classics our readers have grown to love. This year, we're launching several exciting new initiatives, including redesigning the Howell Book House logo and revamping our biggest pet series, Your Happy Healthy Pet™, with bold new covers and updated content. From bringing home a new puppy to competing in advanced equestrian events, Howell has the titles that keep animal lovers coming back again and again.

Contents

Shopping List

You'll need to do a bit of stocking-up before you bring your new dog or puppy home. Below is a basic list of some must-have supplies. For more detailed information on the selection of each item below, consult Chapter 5. For specific guidance on what grooming tools you'll need, review Chapter 7.

☐ Food dish　　　　　　　　☐ Nail clippers

☐ Water dish　　　　　　　　☐ Grooming tools

☐ Dog food　　　　　　　　☐ Chew toys

☐ Leash　　　　　　　　　　☐ Toys

☐ Collar　　　　　　　　　　☐ Flea, tick, and heartworm preventives

☐ Crate　　　　　　　　　　☐ Toothbrush and toothpaste

☐ Crate bedding　　　　　　☐ ID tag

There are likely to be a few other items that you're dying to pick up before bringing your dog home. Use the following blanks to note any additional items you'll be shopping for.

☐ _____

☐ _____

☐ _____

☐ _____

☐ _____

☐ _____

☐ _____

☐ _____

☐ _____

☐ _____

☐ _____

☐ _____

Pet Sitter's Guide

We can be reached at (___)_____-_____ Cellphone (___)_____-_____

_____

We will return on _____ (date) at _____ (approximate time)

Dog's Name _____

Breed, Age, and Sex _____

Spayed or Neutered? _____

Date last heartworm preventive given _____

Date last flea and tick preventive given _____

Important Names and Numbers

Vet's Name _____ Phone (___)_____-_____

Address _____

Emergency Vet's Name _____ Phone (___)_____-_____

Address _____

Poison Control _____ (or call vet first)

Other individual to contact in case of emergency _____

_____

Care Instructions

In the following three blanks let the sitter know what to feed, how much, and when; when the dog should go out; when to give treats; and when to exercise the dog.

Morning _____

Afternoon _____

Evening _____

Water instructions _____

Exercise instructions _____

Medications needed (dosage and schedule) _____

_____

Any special medical conditions _____

_____

Grooming instructions _____

_____

My dog's favorite playtime activities, quirks, and other tips_____

_____

_____

Part I

The World of the Miniature Schnauzer

The Miniature Schnauzer

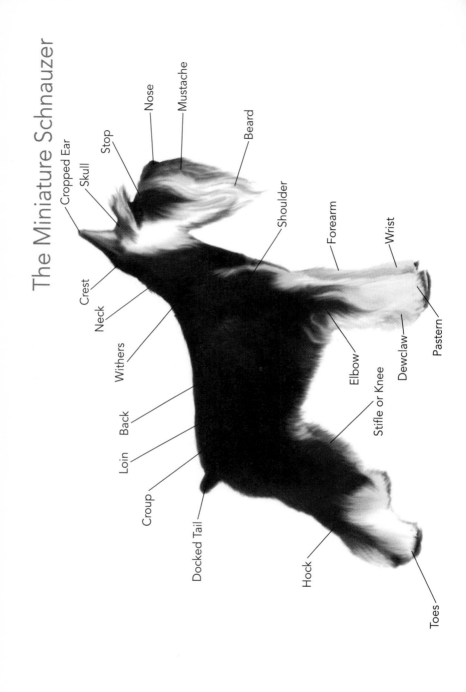

Chapter 1

What Is a Miniature Schnauzer?

When most people see a dog, the word *mustache* seldom crosses their mind. But look at a Miniature Schnauzer, and all that hair covering his upper lip is one of the first things you notice. Here is one very impressive canine mustache! Add his thick-fringed silver beard and wiry gray body, and the Miniature Schnauzer resembles a very distinguished gentleman. All that's missing is a top hat.

This gentleman of a dog turns heads wherever he goes. He's affectionate without being overbearingly gushy; highly intelligent with some degree of independence; extremely curious but not destructive; elegant but hardy; highly protective yet small in size; and equipped with the bonus of all bonuses, a coat that needs some grooming but doesn't shed much and doesn't have a strong doggy odor.

The Miniature Schnauzer shares his aristocratic looks and German origin with the Giant Schnauzer and the Standard Schnauzer (who are in the Working Group). Terriers are tenacious, fast moving, and quick to respond. All three Schnauzers are separate breeds, with the Standard being the oldest of the three and the Miniature being the smallest.

A Small, Versatile Terrier

Besides his upbeat attitude and sturdy, compact size, the Miniature Schnauzer has several other consistent characteristics. These traits are the reason why a Miniature Schnauzer is a unique breed and not just a scaled-down version of the Standard and the Giant Schnauzers.

He's much more than a dog with a pretty face (or an interesting-looking mustache and beard)! The Miniature Schnauzer is hardy and was originally bred to be a companion who could double as a small working farm dog. Although the Standard Schnauzer is a working dog and the Miniature is a terrier, the Miniature Schnauzer inherited from his Standard relative the desire to help his owner around the farm.

This versatile job description meant fetching, carrying, and guarding possessions for the farmer as needed. Pulling and protecting the farm produce cart was one of his responsibilities. Like other terriers, the Miniature Schnauzer's biggest job was keeping the rodent population down.

The Miniature Schnauzer is very versatile, and conscientious breeders are dedicated to making sure he keeps his special characteristics by following an outline of what this dog should look and act like (called the breed standard). You're selecting this breed precisely because you're drawn to the Miniature Schnauzer's unique appearance and personality. As you prepare to choose this breed, you need to know what the ideal Miniature Schnauzer is all about.

The Mini is still a tenacious little terrier and is happy to be both your working dog and your best friend.

The Ideal Miniature Schnauzer

The Miniature Schnauzer doesn't look the way he does by accident. He's the result of several generations of careful planning by many conscientious breeders who have been following the same design, or breed standard, as closely as possible.

In the next few pages you'll find a description of the ideal dog as outlined in the breed standard. If your Miniature Schnauzer falls a little short of the standard written by the American Miniature Schnauzer Club (AMSC), don't despair. The perfect dog (of any breed) hasn't been born yet. Besides, the dog you'll treasure for years to come doesn't have to be exactly perfect. He just needs to look and act mostly like a Miniature Schnauzer and be the dog of your own dreams.

What Is a Breed Standard?

The breed standard describes the ideal or perfect specimen of a breed. It is written by experts from each breed's national club and approved by members of the club and the registry that recognizes the breed (such as the AKC or UKC). It describes the perfect dog in type, structure, movement, color, and temperament. The standard is a conceptual prototype and does not describe any one specific dog.

Breeders measure their breeding stock against this standard and base their breeding decisions on how their dogs measure up. Their goal is to produce puppies who come as close as possible to the ideal. Dog show judges do the same thing when they judge. They look for the dog who comes the closest to the standard.

The first section of the breed standard gives a brief overview of the breed's history. Then it describes the dog's general appearance and size as an adult. Next is a detailed description of the head and neck, then the back and body, and the front and rear legs. The standard then describes the ideal coat and how the dog should be presented in the show ring. It also lists all acceptable colors, patterns, and markings. Then there's a section on how the dog moves, called *gait*. Finally, there's a general description of the dog's temperament.

Each section also lists characteristics that are considered to be faults or disqualifications in the conformation ring. Superficial faults in appearance are often what distinguish a pet-quality dog from a show- or competition-quality dog. However, some faults affect the way a dog moves or his overall health. And faults in temperament are serious business.

You can read all the AKC breed standards at www.akc.org. If you'd like to see an illustrated standard, take a look at the American Miniature Schnauzer Club's web site at www.amsc.us/standard. There's an excellent slide show with seventeen detailed drawings of the breed.

The standard's description of the Miniature Schnauzer's general appearance depicts no fluffy, cutesy little dog. Rather, he is a handsome fellow and she a classy lady. A puppy easily falls into the little fluff-of-a-dog slot, but those sturdy bones and square body, even at a young age, predict the robust and proportionately impressive adult who somehow replaces the fluff.

His appearance and attitude, clearly identifying him as a terrier, are purely deceptive. He has little, if any, terrier in his background; he simply looks and acts like one.

Those eyebrows, that beard, and his alert and active disposition have placed him in the Terrier Group in the AKC and in Canada, but most registries throughout the world classify him as a Working or Utility dog. Still, when you see him in the Terrier Group at any AKC show, he looks like he belongs there.

Colors

This elegant breed comes in three coat colors: salt and pepper, black and silver, and black. Most of the Miniature Schnauzers you'll see are salt and pepper—shades of gray with a coat that's a mixture of black and white banded hairs with solid black hairs and solid white ones. Over time this color combination fades to light gray on the eyebrows, whiskers, and cheeks, under the throat, inside the ears, across the chest, beneath the tail, on the leg furnishings (the long hair on the beard, eyebrows, legs, and underbody), and inside the hind legs.

If you look closely at one hair from a salt and pepper dog's outercoat, you'll see that it has a repeating horizontal pattern of black-and-white bands. Overall the salt and pepper color is created by these individual patterns.

The black and silver dogs have solid black hair on their head, neck, and body, while the furnishings are silver or white.

Black is the only solid color allowed in the standard for a show dog, and the undercoat and outercoat must be true black. As they age, both the blacks and the black and silvers fade to gray.

The dog on the left is salt and pepper, and the one on the right is black and silver.

Of the three colors of Miniature Schnauzers, only the solid black is permitted to have a small white spot on the chest or a single white hair elsewhere on the body. The salt and pepper and black and silver dogs may not have any white patches or any tan or brown markings.

White Miniature Schnauzers

If a dog is solid white, he is automatically disqualified from the show ring in the United States and Canada. (The Federation Cynologique Internationale [FCI], a worldwide organization that regulates the national registries of many countries, permits white Mini Schnauzers to be shown at dog shows.) Breeders also believe that white Mini Schnauzers should be spayed or neutered so they cannot be bred.

Occasionally you may see an advertisement for a "rare and valuable" white Miniature Schnauzer. According to the American Miniature Schnauzer Club and the Canadian Miniature Schnauzer clubs, the white Mini Schnauzer is no more valuable than any of the other colors and the clubs do not endorse white as an acceptable color choice for show dogs.

Conscientious breeders respect the history of the standard and do not breed these colors. Breeders preserve the breed's characteristics, including the accepted colors, and do not arbitrarily change traits just because they want to or because they find some other color appealing.

Size and Weight

In some breeds, the standard dictates that males and females should be different sizes. With Miniature Schnauzers, both sexes should be within the same height and weight range. Male and female Mini Schnauzers are generally twelve to fourteen inches high at the withers (the top of the shoulder) and weigh between eleven and twenty pounds.

In the show ring, if a Miniature Schnauzer is under twelve inches or over fourteen inches in height, the dog is disqualified. But if you're looking for a great pet, it doesn't matter if the dog is over- or undersized.

The Coat

The Miniature Schnauzer has a double coat with a hard, wiry outer layer and a soft undercoat. This combination of wiry and soft coat gives the breed a distinguished, elegant look that sets him apart from other terriers.

What Is a Breed Club?

Love a Miniature Schnauzer? If so, you may be able to join the American Miniature Schnauzer Club (AMSC) and meet other fans, plus learn more about the breed. The AMSC is the parent organization to twenty-five local Mini Schnauzer clubs through-out the United States. Founded in 1933, it has more than 600 members in the United States, Canada, and other countries.

Belonging to this group adds an extra dimension to owning a Mini Schnauzer. You'll learn about the latest developments in health, care, and training, and enjoy a deeper involvement with the breed.

The AMSC is concerned with everything related to the Mini Schnauzer, including defining the breed standard, conducting national dog shows, and providing educational materials such as a detailed illustrated grooming chart. It also encourages research to improve the breed's health and welfare.

To qualify for membership, applicants need the recommen-dations of two existing members and the approval of the Board of Directors. For information about how to join, contact the AMSC at www.amsc.us.

The wiry coat is not accidental. Historically this is a rugged breed who can perform a variety of tough jobs on a German farm in all types of weather. He needs to have this kind of a coat to protect his skin and to keep him dry.

To keep that wiry texture, individual hairs in the coat need to be stripped out or hand plucked almost every day. If this sounds like too much work, you can simply trim the overall coat with electric clippers and not worry about each hair. It's far easier to take care of this way and will still look very nice. Your dog will have a soft coat, and the overall color will look more blended. The constant clipping lightens the body color. This is because the electric clippers trim off the top layers of banded color, while plucking pulls out the entire strand of hair.

Whether you strip it or clip it, your dog's coat needs to be trimmed once every eight weeks. Otherwise your Miniature Schnauzer will have very long and

This dog sports a cool, clipped coat. Show dogs must have a stiff, wiry coat that requires hand stripping, but pets just need to be kept neat and trimmed.

shaggy hair and he won't have that distinguished, dapper look. You can learn to do the job yourself or you can take your dog to a professional groomer. Groomers won't spend the time to strip the coat, but they will use the electric clippers to trim it down for you.

If you are showing your dog, the standard requires the dog to have a wiry coat and the judge has to feel it to make sure that it is stiff. Even the furnishings should be fairly thick but not silky. The standard does not describe a clipped coat, because a dog with this style of grooming is disqualified from the show ring.

The Well-Groomed Gentleman

There's no debate: A Miniature Schnauzer is not a wash-and-wear dog. Sure, he doesn't shed much, but you still have to give him a bath once every three to four weeks (depending upon how down and dirty he likes to get) and brush or comb him nearly every day to untangle any clumps of hair. His toenails need trimming, his ears and eyes should be cleaned, and his teeth must be brushed.

Let's not forget beard care, either. Every time your dog takes a drink of water, there's going to be some dribbling. You'll probably want to wipe down and dry his beard at least once a day to keep the hair from matting. With the salt and pepper and the black and silver dogs, the beard becomes discolored if it isn't kept dry.

Water isn't the only enemy. As neat as your dog may be, there's bound to be bits of food that cling to the hairs in his beard. They must be combed out, or else your dog will become smelly and unhealthy.

Miniature Schnauzer Shape

The overall outline of the Miniature Schnauzer should be square. This means that when you measure the height of his body from the top of his withers to the ground, it should be the same as his length from his rump to his chest.

His head should be rectangular. The muzzle is large in proportion to the skull. The teeth must meet in a scissors bite (the teeth in the upper jaw slightly overlap those in the lower jaw). The eyes should be small, dark brown, oval, and deeply set with an alert and intelligent expression.

The Miniature Schnauzer's neck should be strong and well arched, blending smoothly into the shoulders.

If his ears are cropped (that means a portion of the ears have been surgically removed), they should have pointed tips. If they're uncropped, they should be V-shaped and folded close to the head.

Miniature Schnauzer Facts

Developed in Germany to be a ratter on farms

Member of Terrier Group

Twelve to fourteen inches tall at the withers

Weighs eleven to twenty pounds

Males and females same height and weight

Colors: salt and pepper, black and silver, black

Ranked in the AKC's top fifteen most popular breeds

Minimal shedding

Needs regular grooming

Good with children

Good jogging or TV partner

Smart, curious, fun-loving, agreeable

Likes to bark—good watchdog

Has few health problems

Life span: ten to fourteen years

What About Cropped Ears?

Miniature Schnauzers are born with V-shaped floppy ears. If the breeder wants them to stand upright with a pointed shape, the ears must be surgically trimmed, or cropped, and firmly taped to support them to stay erect.

Originally the ears of fighting dogs and terriers were cropped to prevent them from being bitten off by other dogs or prey. Today the procedure is performed to alter the dog's appearance for cosmetic purposes only.

Cropping is usually done when the dog is about 16 weeks of age, under general anesthesia. During the healing period the ears must be cared for to prevent infection. If you think you want a Miniature Schnauzer with cropped ears, plan on making a few trips to the veterinarian to care for them until they are completely healed.

Dogs with cropped ears cannot be shown in Great Britain and in some other European countries (where ear cropping is illegal), but it is permitted in the United States.

Personality

The typical Miniature Schnauzer's temperament, as described in the standard, is alert, spirited yet obedient, friendly, and intelligent with a willingness to please his owner. This is the picture of a loyal companion who is ready to be your best friend. He should never be overaggressive or timid.

The breed standard does not require ear cropping, which is for cosmetic purposes only.

When it comes time to choose a Miniature Schnauzer, look for an outgoing, happy, fun-loving puppy or dog. Avoid one who is shy or fearful. A shy dog hasn't been well socialized or well trained and lacks self-confidence. He will be harder to manage and will need an experienced owner who can devote a lot of time and training to him.

A Miniature Schnauzer with a stable personality is far easier to live with and will quickly adapt to his new living conditions without a lot of fuss.

Chapter 2

The Miniature Schnauzer's History

Like most breeds, no one knows exactly when the Miniature Schnauzer was first developed, but Standard Schnauzers appear in pictures as early as the sixteenth century. A famous 1501 tapestry depicts a Schnauzer, and Rembrandt included one in one of his paintings from the 1600s.

What is known is that the Schnauzer family originated in the cattle lands of Germany. All authorities recognize the Standard Schnauzer as the original size and prototype of the Schnauzer family. The common link connecting all theories of Schnauzer ancestry is that stocky drovers' dogs formed the foundation from which the Rottweiler, Doberman Pinscher, and Standard Schnauzer descended in the sixteenth century.

The first Standard Schnauzers are thought to be a result of crosses between the black German Poodle and Gray Spitz with Wirehaired Pinscher stock. Bred for sagacity and fearlessness, this dog was an impressive rat catcher, yard dog, and guard.

While German drovers admired the Standard Schnauzer's appearance, soundness, and power, they needed a larger dog to work cattle, so they developed the Giant Schnauzer—probably from early crosses with

---

The Schnauzer Family

The Miniature is part of the Schnauzer family: the Giant Schnauzer (25.5 to 27.5 inches for males; 23.5 to 25.5 inches for females), the Standard Schnauzer (18.5 to 19.5 inches for males; 17.5 to 18.5 inches for females), and the Miniature Schnauzer (12 to 14 inches for both sexes). Each of the three sizes is a distinct and separate breed.

smooth-coated droving and dairymen's dogs. They then crossed the resulting dogs with rough-haired sheepdogs and, eventually, with the black Great Dane and possibly with the Bouvier des Flandres.

Developing the Miniature

Historians estimate that the Miniature Schnauzer was established in 1859, and in 1899 Miniature Schnauzers were exhibited in dog shows as a distinct breed.

As easy as it might sound, breeding the smallest Standard Schnauzers to one another was not how the Miniature was developed. Instead, small Standard Schnauzers were crossed with Affenpinschers and Poodles. Some authorities also think the toy Gray Spitz, Pomeranians, and Wire Fox Terriers might have contributed to the gene pool.

The Miniature, developed as a stable or farm dog, was used as a ratter and guard dog, though not as a fighter. Because of her small size and happy nature, she was invited to join the family as a companion, as well—with great success. It was an unplanned function, but was highly appreciated and valued.

All breeds of dogs were developed with specific capacities to serve their owners. Breeds whose function was to work had to work; they were not expected to be pets. So the Miniature who became a pet continued to perform her intended duties. If your Miniature Schnauzer is very excited chasing rabbits or squirrels, or adamantly stands her ground against an intruder by barking without stop, she is not being silly or stubborn; rather, she is doing what comes naturally as a ratter and a guardian.

The earliest dogs looked very different than today's Miniature. The stocky structure, terrier-like head, wiry coat, and cropped ears were the same, but the breed was not stylish. A ratter or guard didn't need artful grooming, a richly colored coat, and a profuse beard, eyebrows, and leg furnishings. The early colors ranged from black, yellow, and cream to black and tan. The occasional salt and pepper coat emerged later.

The Affenpinscher (small black terrier) influence seems apparent in the earliest known picture of a Miniature Schnauzer, sketched in

Jocco-Fulda Lilliput, the first Miniature Schnauzer in the German stud book, is shown here in a 1907 sketch.

1907. It depicts an 8-year-old dog, Jocco-Fulda Lilliput, who lived to be 16 and is the first Miniature Schnauzer registered in the Pinscher-Zuchtbuch (the German stud book, commonly referred to as the PZ). That registry, first published by the Pinscher-Klub in 1902, formed a joint registry the Bayerischer Schnauzer-Klub in 1918. (Even in the midst of World War I, dog-involved people remained dog involved!)

The Move to America

A breeder in the United States imported the first Standard Schnauzer in 1905. In 1923, W. D. Goff of Massachusetts imported two Miniature Schnauzers from the kennels of Rudolph Krappatch in Germany. Misfortune struck those imports. The female's two litters did not produce any dogs of note, and the male died, leaving no descendants.

The following year, three females and one male from Krappatch's kennel were imported by Marie Slattery, whose kennel name was Marienhof. Three years later, Slattery imported a 3-year-old male. This dog, Cuno, is credited with having been more effectively influential on the breed's development in the United States than any other imported sire. Not a particularly outstanding dog in every respect, Cuno nevertheless earned his American championship and passed on the few outstanding qualities he did have to his puppies, siring fourteen American champions who produced the same fine qualities for many generations.

Intrigued by Slattery's early Miniature imports, other Americans imported 108 dogs and bitches during the following decade. This seems like a lot, but the fact is that most of the lines died out and additional dogs were imported just as pets and were not registered or bred as part of a conscientious breeding program.

Marie Slattery, of Marienhof kennel, imported the early influential Minis from Germany. From left to right, Ch. Handsome of Marienhof, Ch. TMG of Marienhof, and Ch. Kubla Khan of Marienhof.

Two Great Dogs

Amsel, one of Slattery's original imported females, made an astonishing contribution to the breed. She was the first Miniature to be shown in the United States, the dam of the first American-born registered litter (born in 1925), and the great-grandmother of Ch. Moses Taylor, the first American-bred champion. (Moses Taylor actually tied with

Don v. Dornbush as the first American-bred champion, because they earned their titles on the same day at different shows.)

But Amsel's place in history lies in the large number of times her name appears in the pedigrees of top American-bred Miniature Schnauzers. It's an indication that her genetic propensity for producing offspring of superior quality was overwhelming.

Ch. Dorem Display had an outstanding show record and sired forty-two champions.

Any reference to the Miniature Schnauzer must include another great dog, Ch. Dorem Display, a male born on April 5, 1945, and bred by Dorothy Williams at her Dorem Kennels. He was a true terrier, and even today would be a more than worthy contender in the show ring.

Two familiar names crop up on Display's pedigree, too: His ancestry goes back to a litter sired by Cuno and whelped by Amsel.

A Club of Their Own

At first, Standard and Miniature Schnauzers were not recognized as separate breeds. Both were known as Wirehaired Pinschers, and in 1925 the Wirehaired Pinscher Club of America was formed. But a year later the name of both the club and the breed was changed to Schnauzer and the Miniature was recognized by the AKC as a separate breed. The following year, Standards and Miniatures were moved from the Working Group to the Terrier Group.

The Schnauzer Club of America split into two clubs in 1933: the Standard Schnauzer Club of America and the American Miniature Schnauzer Club. In 1945 the Standards moved back to the Working Group.

A New Look

From time to time, breeders change the description of what the ideal dog of a particular breed should look like. The Miniature Schnauzer's original size was a maximum of twelve inches, and between 1930 and 1945 ear cropping was forbidden. Personal preferences toward making the breed more stylish led to breeding for luscious furnishings and darkening the pepper coloration to create a sharper contrast in the salt and pepper coats. Those changes, however, softened the ideally hard texture of the coat, and a sleeker, terrier-type style of Miniature emerged in the late 1940s.

What Is the AKC?

The American Kennel Club (AKC) is the oldest and largest pure-bred dog registry in the United States. Its main function is to record the pedigrees of dogs of the breeds it recognizes. While AKC registration papers are a guarantee that a dog is purebred, they are absolutely not a guarantee of the quality of the dog—as the AKC itself will tell you.

The AKC makes the rules for all the canine sporting events it sanctions and approves judges for those events. It is also involved in various public education programs and legislative efforts regarding dog ownership. More recently, the AKC has helped establish a foundation to study canine health issues and a program to register microchip numbers for companion animal owners. The AKC has no individual members—its members are national and local breed clubs and clubs dedicated to various competitive sports.

Gaining Admirers

Interest in obedience competition greatly increased in 1946, introducing the Miniature Schnauzer to the general public. As the breed improved, more won ribbons at dog shows, as well. Champion (Ch.) Dodi Dimitri was the first Miniature Schnauzer to win Best in Show at the prestigious Montgomery County dog show in 1955, and that same year a brace of two Miniature Schnauzers won Best Team in Show at the Westminster Kennel Club Show. As the number of Group placements and Best-in-Show wins increased, more people began to notice and admire the plucky Miniature.

The number of Miniature Schnauzer breeders and owners increased, and a few even became famous. Four Elfland Kennels Miniature Schnauzers (bred by Florence Bradburn from Temple City, California) appeared in the 1955 movie *It's a Dog's Life*. And Bob Hope invited Walter's Enchanted Echo to appear as a guest on his NBC television show in 1974.

As the breed's popularity soared, the salt and pepper coat became (and continues to be) the most popular color. The number of blacks and black and silvers also increased as the breed gained favor.

The Miniature Schnauzer's climb from obscurity was slow, but in the 1970s it made it to the top ten list of most popular breeds, which is calculated by the number of puppies registered by the AKC. It remained in the top ten for a number of years. In 2004, 24,080 Miniature Schnauzers were registered with the AKC, ranking it the eleventh most popular breed.

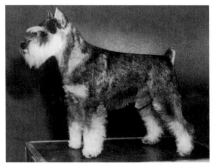

American and Canadian Ch. Jonaire Pocono Rough Rider, UDT, in 1959.

The Price of Popularity

A conscientious breeder becomes nervous when the breed nears the number one spot in popularity. That's because the ranking creates demand for more puppies. Here is where pet stores and puppy brokers see a chance to make money, and they contract with sellers to provide puppies for them. Why isn't this a good way to sell puppies? More puppies mean more breeders, but not all breeders have the same goals in mind.

While reputable breeders are very careful to breed only the best dogs because they want to keep improving the health and appearance of the breed, there are unscrupulous people who are more concerned with making money and see the popularity as an opportunity to produce quantity rather than quality puppies. This can be the downfall for any breed, because the health and welfare of the dams and their puppies are sacrificed in order to turn a profit.

Instead of waiting until the pups are 12 weeks old and physically and emotionally ready to go to their new homes as reputable breeders do, profit-making breeders sell pups days after they are barely weaned, at three or four weeks of age. This is too early for the pups to successfully bond with their littermates, learn from their mothers, or receive enough handling and personal attention from the breeders, all necessary for mature development.

While reputable breeders carefully screen potential buyers to make sure they can provide the right home for a Miniature Schnauzer, disreputable breeders, pet stores, and puppy brokers sell to anyone, with little regard for whether they will make good owners. Conscientious breeders consider it their responsibility to look after all the dogs they sell, and they are eager to help buyers with any health, training, or care problems that come up throughout the dog's lifetime. With retail establishments, the story is different. Once the dog is sold, the

Popularity has been a mixed blessing for the Miniature Schnauzer.

vendors are done helping the customer. Often the dogs are purchased on a whim because the breed is popular; these owners don't realize at the time how much care and training Miniature Schnauzers require. Soon many dogs are neglected or no longer wanted, and a good number are taken to shelters.

To safeguard the Miniature Schnauzer, members of the American Miniature Schnauzer Club are dedicated to caring for the breed. They provide information about health, training, and behavior, and have been instrumental in rescuing any Miniature Schnauzers whose owners can no longer care for them.

Chapter 3

Why Choose a Miniature Schnauzer?

The Miniature is the most popular of the three Schnauzer sizes. It's hard to go anywhere without seeing this bright-eyed dog about town. What do people like about him? Here's a dog with personality plus, who's comfortable in an apartment or a large home, is loyal to his owner, and hardly sheds! If you're looking for an intelligent, playful, yet versatile dog, this breed fits the bill.

While a Miniature Schnauzer has many appealing characteristics, he also has many needs. You have to decide whether this is the right breed for you and your lifestyle before you get one. Unfortunately many people get a dog and find out later that they don't really like him or don't have the time or room for a dog, so they drop him off at a shelter. Every year many Miniature Schnauzers are abandoned. You want your dog to be your lifelong loving companion. Let's start off with some questions.

Is a Mini Right for You?

What first attracted you to this breed? Did you see a Miniature Schnauzer in a dog show or a TV commercial? Were you drawn to his jaunty attitude? Were you intrigued by his comical Groucho Marx eyebrows and his compact size? Choosing a dog shouldn't only be about the way he looks. There's a personality beneath that cute face that you'll have to live with, so make sure it's the one you want.

Whatever the reason, learn as much as you can about this terrier before you bring one home. Getting any dog is a big decision. Sure he's fun, but he's also a

Sure they're cool and funny, but looks shouldn't be the only reason you choose a breed.

24/7 responsibility. It may seem like a good idea to have a dog now, but this is a twelve- to fifteen-year investment of your time, money, and freedom.

Time and Money

Do you have enough time to keep this energetic dog happy? If he's the only dog in your home and you're at work all day, expect him to be bursting with energy when you walk in the door. Maybe all you want to do after a hard day at the office is hang out on the couch. Your Mini Schnauzer has been waiting for you all day, and now he wants to do things. You'll have to play with him, no matter how tired you feel.

Finding a professional dog walker or a good doggy daycare facility that provides activities for your dog while you're away will relieve some of his boredom. Like to go away for the weekends? Unless you plan to take your dog with you, you'll need a pet sitter or you'll have to board him at a kennel, and this is expensive.

Dogs are expensive in other ways, too. The initial price of buying a dog is far less than what you'll spend for the next twelve to fifteen years. Aside from the routine costs of food, toys, grooming, and regular veterinary care, there are supplies to buy, an environment to keep clean and secure, and incidental expenses like training classes, registration and licenses, and flea products. Plus, there will be veterinary emergencies. Does a Miniature Schnauzer fit into your budget?

Space and Mess

What about having enough room for a dog? While your Mini Schnauzer doesn't need a lot of room, he does need a place to eliminate outdoors and some room to run. If you don't have a secure fenced-in yard, you'll need to take him out several times a day. Do you have the patience and energy for that?

Having a dog also means some doggy upkeep. While Mini Schnauzers don't shed much, your dog will need daily brushing and monthly clipping. Do you feel comfortable doing that? If not, can you afford to take him to a groomer to get the job done?

An Eager Learner

Your dog will need some training. Besides housetraining and crate training, you'll need to teach your dog how to walk nicely on the leash, how to sit and stay when you ask him to, and how to behave around visitors. Do you have the time and patience to work with your dog?

One advantage you'll have is that a Miniature Schnauzer really likes to learn. After one training session, he'll look forward to the next because he likes a challenge. The TTT (Typical Terrible Terrier) syndrome doesn't apply to the Miniature Schnauzer. While many terrier breeds may be feisty when you ask them to do something they don't want to do, you don't have to worry about your Miniature Schnauzer reacting like that. Occasionally he may just flatly

All dogs will make a mess. Are you ready to cope with that?

refuse to do what you want right away. But take heart! Eventually he will get around to the command.

What About Smarts?

Do you want a dog who's smart? Before you think a smart dog is an easy dog to train, you should know that in dog lingo, "smart" often means being able to outthink his owner. Training a Mini Schnauzer sometimes means convincing him that *he's* the one who wants to learn the new behavior. Is this something you want to take on?

The Miniature Schnauzer enjoys life because he can amuse himself. He's smart and he knows it. He recognizes your moods and knows when outsmarting you will make you laugh and when it'll get him into trouble. In essence, your Miniature Schnauzer knows he can get away with just about anything because he's amusing, tough, eye-catching, clever, and knows how to handle you.

Understanding Natural Instincts

What about barking? Do you think you can live with a dog who barks?

When it comes to protecting his environment, a Miniature Schnauzer is doing what comes naturally. He was originally bred to be a ratter, and his instincts for alerting you to intruders—both big and small—are sharp. He's a vocal guard dog and can be an extremely insistent barker. This is no half-hearted canine alarm system or a soft-spoken dog at play. Here's a terrier who considers salespeople, delivery services, and visitors as intruders.

If you want a watchdog, this is a valuable trait. But if not, it will take your understanding attitude and effective training to channel your dog's energy. You'll need to train him that it's OK to bark a little when the mail carrier arrives, but to stop when you give the word. Certainly he's allowed to bark, but the volume and objective must not be irritating or disturb the neighbors. Some communities have strict policies about dogs barking after a certain hour. You want your dog to be a good citizen and not cause a nuisance, so be mindful of the noise he makes. Are you up for the challenge?

The Non-Terrier Terrier

If you're looking for a dog you can depend on to stay by your side without a leash when you're outdoors, this breed may not be for you. Remember that his original job was to chase rats away from the farm. If your dog was loose outside and a squirrel ran by, there's no telling how far your dog might run to catch it.

The Dog's Senses

The dog's eyes are designed so that he can see well in relative darkness, has excellent peripheral vision, and is very good at tracking moving objects—all skills that are important to a carnivore. Dogs also have good depth perception. Those advantages come at a price, though: Dogs are nearsighted and are slow to change the focus of their vision. It's a myth that dogs are color-blind. However, while they can see some (but not all) colors, their eyes were designed to most clearly perceive subtle shades of gray—an advantage when they are hunting in low light.

Dogs have about six times fewer taste buds on their tongue than humans do. They can taste sweet, sour, bitter, and salty tastes, but with so few taste buds it's likely that their sense of taste is not very refined.

A dog's ears can swivel independently, like radar dishes, to pick up sounds and pinpoint their location. Dogs can locate a sound in $6/100$ of a second and hear sound four times farther away than we can (which is why there is no reason to yell at your dog). They can also hear sounds at far higher pitches than we can.

In their first few days of life, puppies primarily use their sense of touch to navigate their world. Whiskers on the face, above the eyes, and below the jaws are sensitive enough to detect changes in airflow. Dogs also have touch-sensitive nerve endings all over their bodies, including on their paws.

Smell may be a dog's most remarkable sense. Dogs have about 220 million scent receptors in their nose, compared to about 5 million in humans, and a large part of the canine brain is devoted to interpreting scent. Not only can dogs smell scents that are very faint, but they can also accurately distinguish between those scents. In other words, when you smell a pot of spaghetti sauce cooking, your dog probably smells tomatoes and onions and garlic and oregano and whatever else is in the pot.

Your dog wants to be where you are, indoors or out.

To keep your dog safe, it's best to keep him in a securely fenced yard or on a leash when you're in an unfenced area outdoors.

Playtime!

If you'd like to have a dog who amuses himself and entertains you at the same time, a Miniature Schnauzer might be the breed for you. Armed with a toy, he'll keep himself occupied endlessly. If he's toyless, he'll manufacture a game. A moving shadow on the floor (as tree limbs sway outside on a breezy day) offers paw-pouncing challenges; a housefly elicits a superb degree of eye-darting and air-chomping; the click of temperature-changing appliances (the refrigerator or air conditioner) requires his attentive watchfulness for the next click—he dares it to fail.

It is a wonder, with his innate curiosity and busy attitude, that the Miniature Schnauzer isn't hyperactive. He's not. He knows how to balance the busy times with the down times. And above all, he'll be a delight for years to come. Are you ready?

Chapter 4

Choosing Your Miniature Schnauzer

Congratulations! You've made the commitment to add the pitter-patter of little Miniature Schnauzer paws to your life. Hopefully, you've visited a few dog shows, talked to breeders, owners, and rescue group coordinators, and you've picked up a few grooming tips and have some leads on what to look for in the ideal puppy or dog.

You have several choices to make. Do you want to buy your terrier from a reputable breeder or adopt one from a Mini Schnauzer rescue organization? Does it matter if you have a male or a female? Would you prefer a Mini Schnauzer puppy, adolescent, or adult? If your heart is set on a puppy, are you hoping for a show-quality prospect or a pet? (Both are equally loveable.) What color are you considering—solid black, black and silver, or salt and pepper? Decisions, decisions, decisions.

When looking for the Miniature Schnauzer of your dreams, patience is definitely a virtue. Whether you buy from a breeder or adopt from a rescue organization, the exact age, sex, and color of the dog you want may not be available on the day you want to bring a dog home. Reputable breeders don't breed often, so they keep a waiting list of prospective owners. Rescue groups never know what dogs they will receive.

That's OK. You're going to have your dog for many years to come, so waiting a few weeks or months for the right dog is worth it. Whatever you decide, remember that a new Miniature Schnauzer is a full-time adventure!

Buying from a Breeder

When you buy a Miniature Schnauzer from a reputable breeder, you're not only getting a puppy, you're getting the breeder's years of experience as well. Rather than just breeding dogs to make a profit, this person has a long-time commitment to producing healthy and stable Mini Schnauzers who are good representatives of the breed. The breeder knows the latest health developments and will be eager to share that information with you, and answer any questions you ever have about your dog throughout her lifetime.

You also know what you're getting when you buy a Miniature Schnauzer from a breeder. Whether there's a large kennel of Mini Schnauzers or just a few dogs, the breeder keeps records of every breeding and accumulates information about the sires and dams, often going back several generations.

A reputable breeder socializes her puppies from an early age, so they are used to all kinds of sights, sounds, smells, and people.

The breeder should be very willing to show you the sire and dam and any other relatives of the Miniature Schnauzer you're interested in who may be on the premises, and where the dog has spent most of her time. If you like the way the dog's relatives look and act, plus see a clean, enriching environment, it's a good sign that you're buying a quality dog.

A conscientious Miniature Schnauzer breeder is very willing to answer any questions you have about the dog before you buy her, but be prepared! The breeder will want to ask you several questions about why you're interested in getting this terrier, and how much you already know about the breed. It's OK. The breeder just wants to make sure you will be giving the dog a good home and will care for her for the rest of her life.

Finding a Good Breeder

How do you find a reputable breeder? The AMSC web site (www.amsc.us) has a list of its members who are breeders. These breeders agree to adhere to the list governing rules, which are posted on the web site. You can also check the AKC web site (www.akc.org), or ask your veterinarian, friends who have dogs, members of a local kennel club, or breeders at a dog show for the names of breeders they recommend.

Once you have a list of breeders, interview them by asking a few questions: why they breed, what their experience with the breed is, what health problems appear in the dogs they breed (if the answer is "none" you may want to walk away, because *every* breeder sees some health problems occasionally), what kind of a health guarantee they offer (ask to read it *before* you buy), if they have the puppy or dog's registration papers and can show you a three-generation pedigree.

Ask, too, if this person is willing to show you how to groom your Miniature Schnauzer. And finally, ask whether they're available to take the dog back and properly care for her, if for any reason you can no longer keep her. Through your questions you'll form an opinion about this person and whether you feel comfortable buying a dog from them. Chances are that if you like the breeder, you'll probably like the puppy, adolescent, or adult dog they are offering.

Why Not Buy from a Pet Store?

The only advantage to buying a Miniature Schnauzer from a pet store is that you can have a puppy the day you walk in. There are many disadvantages. A pet store does not sell adults or rehome abandoned dogs. They're selling Miniature Schnauzers strictly to make a profit.

Male or Female?

Other than the obvious anatomy, there is very little difference between male and female Miniature Schnauzers. Emotionally, males and females can be equally gentle, loving, and curious. Physically, males are somewhat more sturdily built than females, with heavier bone structure and thicker coats. Unless you have a show dog, both sexes should be spayed or neutered, so you don't have to worry about reproductive differences.

You'll also pay a lot more than you would from a breeder, you won't be able to see where or how the dog was raised, you're unable to meet the dog's relatives to see if they are the kinds of dogs you would want to have, and you won't know the dog's health history. Pet store employees won't be able to show you how to groom your dog and won't be able to answer any questions you have as the years go by. And if you have to rehome the dog, a pet store will never take her back.

Adopting from a Rescue Group

There are many good puppies, adolescents, and adult Miniature Schnauzers available through Miniature Schnauzer rescue organizations and your local shelters. You have to be patient because a Miniature Schnauzer who fits your criteria may not be available right away. That's OK. Most Miniature Schnauzer clubs have dedicated members who are very anxious to help match you with a dog who needs a home. If they don't have a dog for you when you call, many groups will try to track one down for you in another area or keep your name on a waiting list.

The advantages of acquiring a rescued Mini Schnauzer is that you're giving a deserving dog a home and receiving the support of dedicated Mini Schnauzer lovers who will give you lots of information about health, grooming, behavior, and training for the rest of the dog's life.

Finding a Rescue Group

Finding a Miniature Schnauzer rescue group is easy. The AMSC web site has a rescue group, and you can find many local breed rescue groups online. Most breeders have contact information for rescue groups in their areas, and many shelters can refer you to breed rescue. Each rescue group is independent and the adoption policies vary somewhat from group to group.

Before Mini Schnauzers are ready for adoption they are checked by a veterinarian, given all vaccines, spayed or neutered, and tested for heartworms and any other medical conditions. A behavior expert in the group evaluates each rescue dog to make sure she has a stable personality. There is usually a small fee to adopt, but it hardly ever covers the ongoing costs of the rescue operation.

Adoption can take as little as several days or as long as several months (particularly if there are health issues involved). From the time a dog is placed in a foster home until she is formally adopted usually takes about two to three weeks.

Puppy, Adolescent, or Adult?

If you can't decide whether you want a puppy, an adolescent, or an adult, know that each age has its pros and cons. Just think "time." Consider how much time you have to devote to training each of these age groups.

Puppies are ready to go home after 8 weeks of age. They're easier to acquire than adolescents or adults, but reputable breeders frequently hold on to show-prospect puppies so they can see if the dog is show material. During the first year of puppyhood, you'll be monitoring your Miniature Schnauzer 24/7. There's housetraining, socializing, learning how to groom, and keeping an eye on her all the time to make sure she doesn't destroy anything.

If the young dogs aren't going to be shown, the breeder will spay or neuter them and place them in a good pet home. With adolescent dogs (6 to 12 months old), you'll miss the cute and cuddly puppy stage, but the dog should be housetrained by this age and have had some training. Hopefully, she's been introduced to the world and has been groomed a few times. You'll still need to be on the lookout for teething accidents and monitor your dog's activities at this age.

Adults have lost the puppy look and may not want to cuddle on your lap all the time, but they are housetrained, are finished teething, should be socialized, and should take strangers and the noise and commotion of a busy street for granted. They've been groomed many times and don't require as much supervision.

While puppies can be taught to avoid bad habits from the start, adolescents and adults may have some training issues to correct, but they're very capable of learning whatever it is you want to teach them. The old adage "You can't teach an old dog new tricks" is completely wrong. You can teach a dog to do *anything* at *any age.*

With puppies, there's a lot of speculation about how they'll look when they grow up, but with adolescents and adults, what you see is what you get. Puppies are usually the most expensive of the three age groups, as well. That's because some breeders are so anxious to find a great pet home for an adolescent or an older dog, or maybe even a retired show dog, that they sell the dog at a reduced rate.

> **TIP**
>
> If there are children or other pets in the home, you should always supervise them around your Miniature Schnauzer, no matter how old your dog is.

At four and a half weeks, this pup is not ready to be away from her mother and littermates.

To Show or Not to Show?

A breeder will designate a Miniature Schnauzer puppy as either a show prospect or a pet-quality companion. Pet dogs may have a disqualification that means they can't be shown in the conformation ring, or the dog may have one or more characteristics that don't meet the breed standard. Maybe the dog's coat is too soft, she has an improper bite, or is too large or too small to show. Of course, this doesn't mean she is any less desirable as a companion.

Know What You Need to Show

If you decide that you want a show dog, it's a good idea to spend time with the dog's breeder to find out everything you need to do. There's a lot. Know what you're getting into before you begin. The breeder may require you to show the dog and might ask you to sign an agreement to do so. If you don't know much about showing but want to have a Miniature Schnauzer with a Ch. in front of her name, there's a lot to learn.

For one thing, grooming a Miniature Schnauzer show coat is an extensive and intricate procedure, and it requires a lot of time, talent, and effort. Handling a dog in the ring also requires some flair, some know-how, and some training. Exhibiting a dog in the conformation ring can be costly, time-consuming, physically exhausting, and, more often than not, heartbreaking to a newcomer.

On the other hand, it's a fascinating sport, and nothing beats the high of a big win. If nothing else, it's proof of your dog's relationship to perfection.

If you are determined to have a fling in the ring with your show-quality dog, by all means give it a try. Learn all you can from the dog's breeder, who should be very anxious to help you. Seek advice and help from an expert groomer of the breed and an experienced handler, and start making some friends in the dog fancy. Attend conformation classes with your dog and, most of all, have fun with her.

Your first step is to study the breed standard thoroughly and be honestly convinced that you and your dog belong in the conformation ring. For the dog who is not show quality, obedience and agility training are fun and will bind you and your dog like no other activity. Competing in the obedience and agility rings are fun, especially since Miniature Schnauzers are quick to learn and enjoy these sports.

The Bottom Line

Even if your dog never wins any ribbons, she'll still be thrilled to see you when you come home and love nothing better than snuggling up to you while you're watching TV. It doesn't matter what sex or color your Miniature Schnauzer is, or whether you bought or adopted her when she was a puppy, an adolescent, or an adult. Years later she'll still be your main squeeze.

Show quality or pet quality, your Miniature Schnauzer will be the love of your life.

Part II

Caring for Your Miniature Schnauzer

Chapter 5

Bringing Home Your Miniature Schnauzer

Congratulations! You've made the decision to add a Miniature Schnauzer to your life and now you're ready to welcome the new member of your family into your home. The first few days and weeks of having a new dog are fun and exciting, so keep your camera handy to capture all of those first magic moments.

Naturally, you'll want your Miniature Schnauzer's transition from his former home to your household to be a smooth one. And with just a little advance planning on your part, you can make this happen. Here's your to-do list: Buy some pet supplies, doggy-proof your environment, and choose a good veterinarian. It's amazing how one little Miniature Schnauzer requires so much in the beginning, but the effort will be well worth it in the long run. This dog will be with you for many years to come, so it's a good idea to start off on the right paw.

Shopping for Your Dog

Shopping for dog stuff is the fun part about getting a Miniature Schnauzer, but buyer beware! The cost of pet supplies adds up quickly, so you may want to shop around. Today there are many places that carry the things your dog needs. Check out discount warehouse and pet supply stores, dog catalogs, and the Internet.

One suggestion: Have the basic items, such as a pet carrier and bedding, baby gates, food, water and food dishes, and a few toys on hand *before* your dog

Mini Schnauzer Essentials

You'll need to go shopping *before* you bring your new Miniature Schnauzer home. There are many, many adorable and tempting items at pet supply stores, but these are the basics.

- **Food and water dishes.** Look for bowls that are wide and low or weighted in the bottom so they will be harder to tip over. Stainless steel bowls are a good choice because they are easy to clean (plastic never gets completely clean) and almost impossible to break. Avoid bowls that place the food and water side by side in one unit—it's too easy for your dog to get his water dirty that way.
- **Leash.** A six-foot leather leash will be easy on your hands and very strong.
- **Collar.** Start with a nylon buckle collar. For a perfect fit, you should be able to insert two fingers between the collar and your pup's neck. Your dog will need larger collars as he grows up.
- **Pet carrier.** Choose a sturdy pet carrier (also called a crate) that is easy to clean and large enough for your puppy to stand up, turn around, and lie down in.
- **Nail cutters.** Get a good, sharp pair that are the appropriate size for the nails you will be cutting.
- **Grooming tools.** See chapter 7 for advice on what to buy.
- **Sweater or raincoat.** Despite his double coat, your dog can still catch a chill in very cold weather.
- **Toys.** Watch for sharp edges and unsafe items such as plastic eyes that can be swallowed. Many toys come with squeakers, which dogs can also tear out and swallow. All dogs will eventually destroy their toys; as each toy is torn apart, replace it with a new one.
- **Chew toys.** Dogs *must* chew, especially puppies. Make sure you get things that won't break or crumble off in little bits, which the dog can choke on. Very hard plastic bones are a good choice.

comes home. This way, instead of worrying about rushing out to get all of the supplies right away, you can focus all your attention on your new companion. In a day or so you can take your dog shopping with you to get a collar that fits properly.

It's tempting to buy everything you see for your dog, but all you really need to do is stock up on the basics and then wait to see what your dog likes for the extras.

Sure, there are lots of extra doggy accessories to drool over that just seem to scream, "Take me to your Schnauzer!" But these can wait a few days until your dog settles in and the household adjusts to a regular schedule.

Baby or Child-Safety Gates

A baby or a child-safety gate works wonders if you want to keep your Mini Schnauzer confined to one or two areas of your home, yet enjoy his company at the same time. A smaller environment is easier to watch if your dog is a chewer or you're housetraining him.

Gates come in all different sizes and materials and can become permanent or temporary. They easily attach to doorframes or walls, and you can remove them once you don't need them. Choose gates that are easy to use and lightweight enough to move around. Baby supply stores, discount stores, pet supply places, and pet catalogs all carry baby or child-safety gates.

Food and Water

Ask the breeder or your dog's former owner or the rescue coordinator what food your dog has been eating. Buy it and have it on hand when your dog comes home. Continue feeding this food for the first few weeks. If you decide to change to a different brand, be sure to gradually mix in the new food with the old one. Each day give your dog a little more of the new food until the old food is gone. If you change to the new food too fast, your dog's digestive system may become upset, causing diarrhea.

To avoid upsetting your dog's digestive system the first few days he's in his new home, give him filtered water to drink instead of water straight from your tap. There are different minerals in different

Get sturdy food and water dishes that can't be tipped over or broken and are easy to wash.

water sources, and your dog needs some time to adapt to your water. Gradually add some of your tap water to the filtered water.

Remember to take a bottle of filtered water with you when you take your dog on outings. Unless you're going to be staying in one place for more than a few weeks, your dog's system won't have enough time to become accustomed to the local water supply.

Types of Toys

Besides being just plain fun, toys are necessary for a puppy's development. They give him acceptable things to chew and chase that will challenge his mind and ease the tension of teething at the same time. While just about everything can be a toy, especially to a puppy, providing your Miniature Schnauzer with a big supply of safe things will keep him away from your shoes and the furniture.

There's no shortage of safe doggy toys to choose from through pet catalogs, the Internet, and pet supply stores. You'll find toys in all shapes, sizes, and materials. There are furry, fuzzy, and rubber playthings, balls and ropes with bells and whistles, toys that squeak and talk, light up, or dispense food with just the right nudge. Stores have whole aisles devoted to any and every kind of chewy bone you can think of.

There are many natural and synthetic bones for dogs that are safe to chomp on. Long leg bones that have been specially processed and smoked are great treats, as long as they don't crack and splinter. Different shapes and sizes of nylon chew bones that smell like real bones are safe for your Miniature Schnauzer.

Toys are not optional. Just be sure you choose safe toys that are the right size for a small dog.

A few cautions: Avoid wood, plastic, and bones that splinter. Stay away from very small toys that your dog can swallow, and keep an eye on things with squeakers because he can choke on them after chewing the toy for a while. Also stay away from all rawhide products and digestible dental chews because after extended chewing these can become lodged in your dog's throat or cause intestinal problems.

Every Mini Schnauzer has his own favorite toys, and there's no way of knowing which ones they are until you buy them. Your dog will decide which toy is more fun with or without your company.

Collars and Leashes

The easiest way to find a collar that properly fits your dog is to take him with you. Choosing a collar may sound simple, but you'll find rows and rows of them for sale. Too many choices can be so overwhelming that you may be tempted to buy one of every type, size, and color. Luckily, your dog only needs one collar that fits him the day you go shopping.

If you have a puppy or a young dog who is still growing, don't buy a collar that's too big for him, thinking he'll grow into it. That may take awhile, and in the meantime if the collar slips off, it's useless. Choose the one that fits your dog now. When it fits properly you should be able to easily get your finger underneath it. The collar should be adjustable so you can expand it as he grows. Frequently check how snug it is to make sure it's not too tight.

When you take your dog out for a walk or when you're training him, you can use a metal, nylon, or fabric slip collar, but don't leave it on him when you're not around. One of the

> **T I P**
>
> It's best to pick up your Miniature Schnauzer early in the morning on the first day of the weekend you're getting him. This gives you the rest of the day and one or two more to really get to know him.

metal rings could catch on something and your dog could choke. If you'd rather use a harness instead of a collar for your dog, that's OK.

In the lead or leash department, forget the chain or retractable leads because they can be dangerous if a dog or person gets tangled in them. Instead, choose a half-inch wide, four- to six-foot-long nylon, cotton-webbed, or leather leash. The leash should feel comfortable in your hands and never awkward to hold. Leather is stiff at first but softens up with use, is easy to grasp, and will last the longest. Sure it's more expensive but it's well worth the cost, because unless your Miniature Schnauzer chews it up, leather will last forever.

Choosing and Using a Pet Carrier

If you've never used a pet carrier before, it may seem like a jail to you. But to your dog, it's home sweet home. Dogs, like their wolf ancestors, feel safe if they're in a denlike cozy retreat, such as a carrier. You'll find many different types and sizes of pet carriers for sale. There are soft-sided fold-ups, collapsible wire models, and solid-sided hard plastic to choose from.

Each has advantages. The soft-sided models are the lightest and easiest to move around from room to room, the wire carriers permit more air to flow through, and the solid-sided carriers are the sturdiest for your dog when he's riding in the car or going for an airplane ride.

The Right Size

What size should you buy? Your Mini Schnauzer should be able to lie down, turn around, and have three to four inches of extra headroom when he's sitting or standing up. The best size may seem too small to you, but it isn't to your dog.

If you have a puppy, buy a carrier that fits him on the day you buy it, but plan on getting a larger one when he's an adult. Or start with the larger carrier to begin with. If you do, you'll need to add a divider panel while he's still small.

Otherwise come bathroom time he'll potty in all that extra space instead of going outdoors—a bad habit you don't want him to get into.

Generally, since male and female Mini Schnauzer adults are the same size (twelve to fourteen inches tall), they will need a crate that's one or two models up from most manufacturers' smallest size.

Bedding

Expensive pet cushions can be monogrammed on your choice of fabrics and even come with special padding, but skip putting something like this into your Mini Schnauzer's carrier right now. Your dog may chew it up and possibly swallow pieces of it, which can be dangerous. When you know that he isn't going to destroy his bedding, you can always add the fancy stuff later on.

In the meantime, give him old comfy blankets to snuggle up with. Your dog's bedding should be soft and washable and big enough to provide padding for the hard carrier bottom.

Using the Carrier

Your dog's first ride home is a good time to begin the habit of putting him inside it whenever he's in the car. In case there's an accident, the carrier provides some protection for him. If a carrier doesn't fit inside your car, the next safest way to transport your Mini is to use a doggy harness that hooks into the car seat belt.

When else should your dog use his carrier? It's perfect for naps, nighttime sleeping, housetraining, a meal from time to time, and for any occasion when you can't keep an eye on him. Unless someone is home to let your dog out of the carrier to go to the bathroom and socialize, don't use it to confine your dog for more than an hour or two during the daytime.

To train your dog to like his carrier, make a game out of giving him a food treat by tossing it inside before putting him in. Praise him for going in after the treat. Then close the door. Don't leave the carrier in another room, because your dog will feel as if he's been left behind in a strange place. Keep it where he can see a family member.

Where to Put It?

At night put it next to your bed. This way, if your dog feels lonely you can reassure him that you are right there. Resist the temptation to take your new dog in bed with you. If you have a puppy there's the chance that you might roll over on him. If you have an adult, you don't know if he's 100 percent housetrained yet. Both the puppy and the adult dog need to adapt to a place all their own. If they

An old washable blanket is a good choice for puppy bedding.

sleep on the bed, they'll end up preferring the bed to the carrier, which isn't a good idea.

The first night your new dog comes home, put a Schnauzer-sized stuffed animal inside the carrier. (First be sure to remove any hard pieces, such as eyes and a nose, that he could swallow!) In his previous home he may have had littermates or another dog to snuggle up against for comfort. Here, alone in a new pet carrier, a big furry toy is the next best thing.

During the daytime, move the carrier into the room you'll spend the most amount of time in. Or if you prefer, buy a second carrier you can leave in the same place all the time.

Puppy-Proofing

With puppies, chewing goes with the territory. When Miniature Schnauzer pups are about 3 weeks old, they begin getting their baby teeth. By 4 to 5 months, these teeth begin to fall out to make room for their permanent adult teeth. To soothe the discomfort of teething, puppies will gnaw or chomp on just about anything they can find—carpet, furniture, personal possessions, leather, and even walls.

Puppy-Proofing Your Home

You can prevent much of the destruction puppies can cause and keep your new dog safe by looking at your home and yard from a dog's point of view. Get down on all fours and look around. Do you see loose electrical wires, cords dangling from the blinds, or chewy shoes on the floor? Your pup will see them too!

In the kitchen:

- Put all knives and other utensils away in drawers.
- Get a trash can with a tight-fitting lid.
- Put all household cleaners in cupboards that close securely; consider using childproof latches on the cabinet doors.

In the bathroom:

- Keep all household cleaners, medicines, vitamins, shampoos, bath products, perfumes, makeup, nail polish remover, and other personal products in cupboards that close securely; consider using childproof latches on the cabinet doors.
- Get a trash can with a tight-fitting lid.
- Don't use toilet bowl cleaners that release chemicals into the bowl every time you flush.
- Keep the toilet bowl lid down.
- Throw away potpourri and any solid air fresheners.

In the bedroom:

- Securely put away all potentially dangerous items, including medicines and medicine containers, vitamins and supplements, perfumes, and makeup.
- Put all your jewelry, barrettes, and hairpins in secure boxes.
- Pick up all socks, shoes, and other chewables.

In the rest of the house:

- Tape up or cover electrical cords; consider childproof covers for unused outlets.
- Knot or tie up any dangling cords from curtains, blinds, and the telephone.

- Securely put away all potentially dangerous items, including medicines and medicine containers, vitamins and supplements, cigarettes, cigars, pipes and pipe tobacco, pens, pencils, felt-tip markers, craft and sewing supplies, and laundry products.
- Put all houseplants out of reach.
- Move breakable items off low tables and shelves.
- Pick up all chewable items, including television and electronics remote controls, cellphones, shoes, socks, slippers and sandals, food, dishes, cups and utensils, toys, books and magazines, and anything else that can be chewed on.

In the garage:

- Store all gardening supplies and pool chemicals out of reach of the dog.
- Store all antifreeze, oil, and other car fluids securely, and clean up any spills by hosing them down for at least ten minutes.
- Put all dangerous substances on high shelves or in cupboards that close securely; consider using childproof latches on the cabinet doors.
- Pick up and put away all tools.
- Sweep the floor for nails and other small, sharp items.

In the yard:

- Put the gardening tools away after each use.
- Make sure the kids put away their toys when they're finished playing.
- Keep the pool covered or otherwise restrict your pup's access to it when you're not there to supervise.
- Secure the cords on backyard lights and other appliances.
- Inspect your fence thoroughly. If there are any gaps or holes in the fence, fix them.
- Make sure you have no toxic plants in the garden.

A Miniature Schnauzer puppy is very small, and it may be difficult to imagine all the trouble he can get into. When you're puppy-proofing your home and yard, get down on the ground and try to look at things from a pup's-eye view.

Older puppies, as well as new adults who are less than about 5 years of age, may continue the habit if they're curious, lonely, bored, or just because an item smells or tastes interesting.

If you want to protect everything in your home, keep an eye on your Mini Schnauzer *all the time!* When you can't watch him, put him in his pet carrier or exercise pen, or in his fenced and safe backyard.

Inspect everything in your home to make sure that if your dog does chew something, he won't damage the item or hurt himself. According to the ASPCA Animal Poison Control Center, substances that can cause mild gastrointestinal upset if your dog ingests them include water-based paints, water in your toilet, silica gel, cat litter, glue traps, jewelry, and Christmas tree water.

Finding a Veterinarian

A good veterinarian will be your dog's next best friend. To find a doctor who is knowledgeable and someone you feel comfortable with, ask your friends and neighbors who have dogs to recommend the veterinarian they visit. You can also call local groomers, members of the nearby kennel club, and your Miniature

Schnauzer's breeder for recommendations, or access a Miniature Schnauzer online message board. The American Veterinary Medical Association's web site at www. avma.org will also have the names of veterinarians in your area.

The First Visit

Within the first 48 hours of bringing your new puppy home, take him to the veterinarian for a checkup. It is important to establish a good rapport with your veterinarian; after all, this is the person you are trusting to take care of your dog for many years to come.

Start your puppy right away with a regular routine for eating, sleeping, playing, and potty breaks.

The doctor will check your Miniature Schnauzer to make sure he is healthy and will give him any vaccinations he needs and a vaccination schedule. Be sure to ask the veterinarian any questions about feeding, training, and behavior that you may have.

When you're at the veterinarian's office, pay attention to how the staff and the vet handle your dog. Is the waiting room clean and comfortable for the animals? Do you have to wait a long time with no explanation? Is the veterinarian interested in answering your questions and does he or she handle your dog well? If you don't get a good feeling about the people or the place, keep looking.

It's your responsibility to be a good patient, too. Train your Miniature Schnauzer to accept handling by the veterinarian. Get him used to the vet's office by taking him in every once in awhile even if he doesn't have an appointment. Let the staff feed him a treat, then just leave.

Chapter 6

Feeding Your Miniature Schnauzer

Most Miniature Schnauzers have never met a food item they didn't love. When the dinner hour rolls around, it doesn't take long before your dog will have bits of watery kibble clinging to her beard, mustache, and eyebrows. If the food is nutritious and your dog likes the recipe, it's a moveable feast.

Water

Water is the single most important nutrient, because without it life ceases to exist. Dogs drink more water than people; therefore, it's important for your dog to have access to fresh water at all times. (The only exception to this is during early puppyhood, when you should take away your puppy's water after her last nighttime walk before bed. That way she won't need to urinate in the middle of the night.)

Choosing a Dog Food

Go to any pet supply store and you'll see rows and rows of commercially prepared dog foods, canned and dry, in a variety of prices, sizes, and flavors. Commercial dog food manufacturers spend millions of dollars researching dogs' nutritional needs so that their products are nutritionally complete and balanced.

Their ongoing research ensures consumers that their products meet the requirements of a public that has become extremely health-conscious, especially when their pets are concerned. If you don't want your Miniature Schnauzer to become a finicky eater, don't feed her steak, twice-baked potatoes, and cherries jubilee. Feed her dog food that is nutritionally complete and balanced.

Types of Foods

Dry food, commonly called kibble, is easy and economical, and a sound nutritional choice for the dog. Kibble contains 18 to 27 percent protein, 7 to 15 percent fat, less than 1 percent water, and about 35 to 50 percent carbohydrates. It's a complete meal and has many advantages. It helps scrape tartar off teeth, is less expensive in the long run because you feed less than canned food, doesn't require refrigeration, and is easy to store or take on vacation.

Canned food contains 8 to 15 percent protein, between 2 and 15 percent fat, and 72 to 78 percent water with some meat and vegetable ingredients. Some canned recipes are complete meals, but others need to be mixed with dry food. Once it's opened, it needs to be refrigerated. It's more expensive to feed on its own, and it stains a Mini's beard. It's not a good idea to feed your Miniature Schnauzer only canned food because it's too soft and tartar tends to build up on your dog's teeth.

Vitamins and minerals can be found in fruits and vegetables, which make excellent snacks for your dog.

Your dog's food is doing its job if she is healthy and in good weight.

What to Buy?

How do you know which kind of dog food to buy? Not the most or least expensive brand or the one you see in every advertisement. Choose a food by reading the label. The ingredients are listed on the bag or can, and you want a food that lists an animal source meat as the protein—such as beef, turkey, chicken, lamb, fish, or duck—as the first ingredient. The second ingredient should be a plant source such as barley, corn, rice, or wheat, and the third ingredient should be another meat source.

There are three categories of dog food: super-premium, premium, and low-cost. The super-premium is usually the most expensive because it has the best-quality ingredients. Your dog doesn't have to eat as much of this type to feel full, because nutritionally speaking, it's very dense. Therefore, the extra cost is not as high as it seems.

The premium foods are less expensive than super-premium and have more artificial ingredients, while the low-cost foods have cheaper ingredients with more fillers. You will have to feed your dog more of these foods to give her the same nutrition. So what seems like a bargain really is not.

Your Miniature Schnauzer's food is doing its job if your dog is healthy, in good weight, and her stools are well formed (not loose or rock hard) and not too big or too small.

Reading Dog Food Labels

Dog food labels are not always easy to read, but if you know what to look for they can tell you a lot about what your dog is eating.

- The label should have a statement saying the dog food meets or exceeds the American Association of Feed Control Officials (AAFCO) nutritional guidelines. If the dog food doesn't meet AAFCO guidelines, it can't be considered complete and balanced, and can cause nutritional deficiencies.
- The guaranteed analysis lists the minimum percentages of crude protein and crude fat and the maximum percentages of crude fiber and water. AAFCO requires a minimum of 18 percent crude protein for adult dogs and 22 percent crude protein for puppies on a dry matter basis (that means with the water removed; canned foods should have more protein because they have more water). Dog food must also have a minimum of 5 percent crude fat for adults and 8 percent crude fat for puppies.
- The ingredients list the most common item in the food first, and so on until you get to the least common item, which is listed last.
- Look for a dog food that lists an animal protein source first, such as chicken or poultry meal, beef or beef by-products, and that has other protein sources listed among the top five ingredients. That's because a food that lists chicken, wheat, wheat gluten, corn, and wheat fiber as the first five ingredients has more chicken than wheat, but may not have more chicken than all the grain products put together.
- Other ingredients may include a carbohydrate source, fat, vitamins and minerals, preservatives, fiber, and sometimes other additives purported to be healthy.
- Some grocery store brands may add artificial colors, sugar, and fillers—all of which should be avoided.

Choose an Eating Area

It doesn't matter where you put your dog's stainless steel food and water dishes, but you should keep them in the same place all the time. Dogs are creatures of habit and they become very attached to their assigned areas. If you feed your dog in different rooms, she may become too confused to eat.

The kitchen and laundry rooms are convenient locations, especially if you're nearby. No one likes to eat alone, including your Miniature Schnauzer. Once you put the bowl down, stick around until she finishes. There's a possibility that if you walk away, she would rather follow you than eat.

Stick to a Schedule

Feed your Mini Schnauzer at the same time every day in the same location. Believe it or not, your dog can tell time. She has a built-in alarm clock (her stomach) that goes off when it's time to dine. If you have a puppy, setting up a regular feeding schedule helps with housetraining because puppies need to eliminate after they eat.

Miniature Schnauzers are eager eaters, so once you put your dog's food bowl down, expect her to finish it. If she eats some of it and walks away, leave the bowl out for only ten minutes, then pick it up and discard the food. Don't give her anything else to eat—including snacks—until it's time for the next regularly scheduled meal. If she eats that meal, great. If not, don't worry.

It's OK if your dog skips one meal. If she turns her nose up at two or three meals, it may mean she's ill and you should call your veterinarian. If there's nothing wrong she'll probably gobble up her food at the next meal.

Do not leave the food out all day long. If you do, you won't be able to tell if your dog has lost her appetite and is ill, or even how much food she has eaten.

Miniature Schnauzers are eager eaters.

How Much to Feed Your Mini Schnauzer

Puppies

Keep a measuring scoop in the dog food so you can measure out exactly how much food your dog is getting. During a puppy's period of intense growth and development, she requires almost twice the amount of most nutrients per pound of body weight as an adult dog needs. And at 6 to 8 weeks of age, a puppy

Avoid Dangerous Foods

Some foods are deadly if your Miniature Schnauzer eats them. These include any type of bones that are likely to splinter—chicken, turkey, pork, or beef bones. Avoid spicy foods, onions, and broccoli, since they may upset your dog's stomach, and skip chocolate altogether because it contains an ingredient that is toxic to dogs. Raisins and grapes have also been found to be dangerous for dogs.

requires at least three times the adult dog's caloric requirements per pound of body weight. Because of these nutritional needs, you should feed your puppy three or four times a day. Ask your dog's veterinarian, breeder, or rescue coordinator how much per meal; you don't want your puppy to eat too much, but you certainly don't want to underfeed her.

Manufacturers of the best brands of dog food have taken all of these requirements into consideration, and since the amounts fed to your puppy gradually decrease over her growth and development period, the decreased caloric ingestion is automatic. During that first intensive year, a nutritional and balanced diet will develop strong bones and teeth, clear eyes, and a healthy coat, and will promote healthy body functions.

While a roly-poly puppy is cute and healthy, don't allow her to become an obese adult by overfeeding and not getting enough exercise. If she does become overweight, gradually decrease the amount of food you give until she's in proper weight, then maintain the proper amount, and make sure she gets plenty of exercise.

Adults

The caloric requirement gradually decreases to twice the adult dog's needs until the puppy is 16 weeks old and continues to gradually decrease, reaching an adult dog's caloric requirement at about 1 year of age. The number of meals you feed will decrease, too, until your puppy is eating one or two meals a day.

Most adult Miniature Schnauzers eat half a cup of dry food in the morning and half a cup in the evening.

TIP

Be sure to wash your dog's bowls every day to avoid bacterial contamination and make sure that fresh, cool water is available at all times.

Pet Food vs. People Food

Many of the foods we eat are excellent sources of nutrients—after all, we do just fine on them. But dogs, just like us, need the right combination of meat and other ingredients for a complete and balanced diet, and a bowl of meat doesn't provide that. In the wild, dogs eat the fur, skin, bones, and guts of their prey, and even the contents of the stomach.

This doesn't mean your dog can't eat what you eat. A little meat, dairy, bread, some fruits, or vegetables as a treat are great. Fresh foods have natural enzymes that processed foods don't have. Just remember, we're talking about the same food you eat, not the gristly, greasy leftovers you would normally toss in the trash. Stay away from sugar, too, and remember that chocolate is toxic to dogs.

If you want to share your food with your dog, be sure the total amount you give her each day doesn't make up more than 15 percent of her diet, and that the rest of what you feed her is a top-quality complete and balanced dog food. (More people food could upset the balance of nutrients in the commercial food.)

Can your dog eat an entirely homemade diet? Certainly, if you are willing to work at it. Any homemade diet will have to be carefully balanced, with all the right nutrients in just the right amounts. It requires a lot of research to make a proper homemade diet, but it can be done. It's best to work with a veterinary nutritionist.

Seniors

As dogs grow, their nutritional needs change. The canine senior citizen is less active and her body begins to slow down. She'll need less food as she ages. Talk to your dog's veterinarian about adjusting her diet as she ages.

Avoid Bad Table Manners

If you're annoyed by the interruption of recorded telephone sales pitches at dinner time, you'll be more annoyed by your dog pestering you during your meals. To avoid her pesky behavior, don't reward it by giving her tidbits from the table. The first time she places her paws on your lap, your immediate reaction must be a stern "off" as you push her away. You're not angry; your attitude is quite matter-of-fact as you continue to eat. She'll probably try again, placing her paws on your lap.

As many times as are necessary, continue to push her away with a stern "off," exhibiting your unchanged attitude until she simply

Make sure you count the training treats when you are figuring how much to feed your dog each day.

gives up. She may try again during that meal or the next or the next, but will only be consistently told "off." Your dog is no dummy, and will quickly learn not to bother you when you eat.

Chapter 7

Grooming Your Miniature Schnauzer

A ll dogs need *some* grooming. Plan on setting aside plenty of time to keep your dog looking good. The Miniature Schnauzer doesn't shed much, but there's still monthly bathing and daily brushing and combing to be done. Don't forget too, that once a week the dog's toenails must be trimmed, his ears cleaned, and his teeth brushed.

Every eight weeks your dog's coat should be clipped. Otherwise your Miniature Schnauzer will have long and shaggy hair and he'll look unkempt. Your pet Miniature Schnauzer doesn't have to look like a show dog, but if you want to keep the harsh coat that show dogs must have, you'll need to hand pluck the hair almost daily. This is a very tedious procedure, but if you don't mind having a dog with a soft coat, you can use electric clippers to quickly buzz off the hair as it grows and your dog will look very attractive.

Here's where a professional groomer comes in handy! This person will do the work of keeping the hair at the right length. The coat still won't feel and look like a show dog's would—only daily hand plucking can do that. But it's perfectly OK for a dog who will not be shown in conformation.

You can also learn how to groom your dog yourself. Your dog's breeder can teach you how to do the job properly and will give you a grooming chart and a list of the tools you need. The American Miniature Schnauzer Club's web site (www.amsc.us) also has information about grooming.

Grooming Equipment

Even though you may decide to have your Miniature Schnauzer groomed by a professional, you'll need to maintain his appearance between visits. That means combing out and cleaning his beard every day and brushing him at least twice a week. One suggestion: While you're brushing out your dog, wear a washable, slick-fabric grooming smock. Schnauzer hair sticks to T-shirts and most other fabrics.

Electric Clippers

If you plan to clip your dog yourself, you'll need scissors and an electric clipper, and you'll have to get the blades sharpened regularly. Coat clippers come in many types, styles, and prices. According to the AMSC web site, the Oster Detachable Blade #A5 clipper and the Andis are the most commonly used brands and models. The blades are detachable and snap into place. Different blades are used to clip different areas of your dog's coat. Choose sizes 10, 30, 40, 15, and 7F (full tooth). The higher the number, the closer the cut. Use the 40 blade for your dog's ears, the 10 for the body, and the 7F for a dog with a thin coat.

To prevent the blade from getting hot when you use it, lubricate it with clipper oil before beginning to clip. These tools are somewhat delicate, and if they're accidentally dropped they may move out of alignment or break, so do be careful.

Grooming Table

If you are going to do the clipping at home, having a grooming table, whether homemade or purchased, will help steady your dog while you're working on him. It will also enable you to raise him to a comfortable height, so you are not always bending over. Your grooming table should have an adjustable arm with a loop of thin leash (called, rather darkly, a noose) to hold your dog's head steady. If you don't have a grooming table, you can put a rubber bathmat or any nonslip surface on a table. Choose a spot for your grooming table that has good lighting so you can see what you're doing up close and personal.

Nail Clippers

When you're shopping for nail clippers, there are two different styles to choose from: scissors and guillotine. The guillotine type is more popular because you cut from the front of the nail and can see across the whole nail. With the scissors you're cutting from the side of the nail. Everyone has a personal preference, though, so you may want to try both models yourself to see which you like. Choose the size for a medium dog.

A grooming table can also be a handy place to bathe your dog outside. Always use a shampoo made for dogs, because shampoos for humans will dry out a dog's coat.

Using a battery-powered nail grinder is another option for trimming. It may seem intimidating to you and your dog because of the noise it makes, but it's actually more efficient and faster to use. A nail grinder is easier to use than nail clippers because you can trim the nails farther back without worrying that you're cutting too close to the quick.

Always have styptic powder handy in case you cut the quick (the bundle of blood vessels and nerves that runs through the center of each nail) and a nail begins to bleed. You'll be cutting a lot of nails throughout the dog's life, and it's inevitable that you'll nip the quick at least once. If so, you can immediately stop the bleeding by applying some styptic powder. (Cornstarch will also do in a pinch.)

Shampoo

To bathe your dog, a kitchen sink, if it's big enough, may work just fine. If not, there's always your shower or your regular bathtub. A handheld sprayer attached to the faucet makes rinsing easier, and be sure to use a quality shampoo especially formulated for dogs. Avoid using human shampoo on your dog because it is too harsh for a Mini Schnauzer's skin and can cause flaking.

Grooming Tools for Miniature Schnauzers

Pin brush
Slicker brush
Metal comb
Large scissors
Small scissors
Thinning shears
Electric coat clipper
Nail clippers or small, battery-operated nail grinder
Styptic powder
Tweezers
Doggy toothbrush and doggy toothpaste
Canine shampoo and conditioner
Grooming table with arm and noose (optional)
Towels
Cotton balls
Rubbing alcohol
Canine or human hair dryer with low setting

To make grooming convenient for you, put all your grooming supplies into a portable container and store them near your grooming table or hang the equipment up on a pegboard next to the table. This way, you'll know where they are when you need them.

Training Your Puppy to Like Grooming

Since grooming will become a daily part of your Miniature Schnauzer's life, training him to feel comfortable and to stand still on a grooming table is a high priority. Even if you take your dog to a professional groomer, you still have to brush him and trim his nails between visits. Putting him on a table makes it easier to see the whole dog and to perform these tasks. And it's easier on your back, too.

TIP

Before beginning any grooming session, be sure to take your dog outside to eliminate.

His first experience on a grooming table should be fun and very positive. Introduce him to the table the first day you bring him home. You're not going to groom him that day, but while holding him, gently place him up there and let him sniff around.

For a little dog, the table is a long way from the ground, so watch that he doesn't slip off. While your dog is on the table, never turn your back on him or leave him unattended! He can easily slip and fall off.

The next day, repeat the trip to the table but give your dog a small food treat. When you think he feels comfortable on the table, begin training him to stand still while being groomed. Hold him up under his tummy while you stroke and softly praise him, saying, "stand." If he wiggles (and he will), patiently continue the procedure for a moment, then stop. If he tries to sit (and he will), gently lift him under his tummy and remind him, "stand." When the puppy stands for a few moments, reward him with a small food treat and praise him by saying, "good boy, good boy!"

Gradually extend the time, but it isn't necessary for him to remain standing for hours. Even an older dog occasionally needs to change his position momentarily. Gradually and patiently teach him to lie on his side to have his legs and underside groomed.

A few days before you actually plan to use the electric clippers, show it to your dog and turn it on so he can become accustomed to the buzzing sound. Let him investigate all of the grooming tools by sniffing them to his heart's content.

Eye Care

Every day, check your Miniature Schnauzer's eyes, because many dogs accumulate a bit of mucus in the corners of their eyes. Use a tissue or cotton ball to remove any

Check your dog's eyes every day. And don't let him hang his head out the window when you're driving, because road dirt and grit can really damage his eyes.

matter, or wipe the area with a product specifically made for eye tearing, then rinse with clear water.

Get in the habit of looking at your dog's eyes and eyelids for any signs of squinting, redness, or swelling. It may mean there's an infection and you'll need to call your veterinarian. It's important to catch the problem early by observing your dog.

Teeth and Gums

Like all dogs, adult Miniature Schnauzers have forty-two permanent teeth; puppies have twenty-three baby teeth with no molars. As each adult tooth emerges, any interfering baby tooth should be removed.

Dog teeth are just like human teeth. If they're not kept clean and bacteria has a chance to accumulate at the gumline, trouble begins. When your dog eats, a layer of thin, sticky bacteria called *plaque* begins to build up. The plaque quickly hardens into tartar—a hard substance that needs to be removed by a veterinarian using special dental instruments.

A buildup of tartar and plaque causes gingivitis and results in gums that are red, sensitive, swollen, and sore. When rubbed, the gums may bleed. Inflamed gums eventually separate from the sides of the teeth, allowing bacteria and food to collect inside, which invites periodontal disease.

If you want your dog to have healthy teeth all his life, and to avoid serious oral infections, the tartar on his teeth must be removed whenever it begins to accumulate.

Some dogs, no matter what they eat, will form more tartar on their teeth than other dogs. Miniature Schnauzers build up tartar very quickly. By the time he's a year old, a Miniature Schnauzer will have a mouth full of tartar that needs to be removed.

The appearance of an adult dog's sparkling white front teeth can be deceptive; her back teeth (and the insides of those front teeth) may have a collection of tartar, causing the gums to swell and possibly become infected, and the teeth to decay.

Dog Breath

If your dog has bad breath, it's probably because he has gingivitis. Dog breath is a sure sign you've neglected your dog's tooth care. If you haven't, and your dog's teeth are healthy, it's a sign of another problem. In either event, you should make an appointment to see your veterinarian.

Brushing Your Dog's Teeth

When your dog is about 6 months old, it's time to start brushing his teeth. It doesn't take more than a few minutes and should be done at least two to three times a week, if not daily. Be sure to use a toothbrush and toothpaste made just for dogs—especially the toothpaste, which has beneficial enzymes that combine with saliva to dissolve plaque. Toothpaste made for humans has a higher level of fluoride and may contain sodium or detergents that are harmful to your dog's teeth. Besides, canine toothpaste tastes much better to a dog and is easier for him to swallow. Don't worry. He doesn't have to rinse!

Canine toothbrushes are smaller than human brushes and fit better in a dog's mouth. You can also use a child's soft toothbrush or a gauze pad wrapped around your finger. Brush your dog's teeth by rubbing the toothpaste along the gum line and over the surface of the teeth.

To reach the areas a toothbrush can't, your veterinarian can thoroughly clean your dog's teeth as needed.

Nail Clipping Tips

If you want your Miniature Schnauzer to have short, healthy nails, trim them once a week. Sure, you can cut them once every two or three weeks, but they will only be longer and the job will take more time. Trimming nails isn't just for beauty. It's a safety issue.

Nails that are too long begin curling over the pads of your dog's feet and even worse, can push into the pads. Overgrown nails can also throw a dog slightly off balance. If you hear your dog's nails click on the floor, they're too long.

Begin trimming your dog's nails as soon as you acquire him. Slowly introduce him to the nail clippers by letting him sniff and see how they work. Then slowly lift one foot, letting it rest on your hand, until he allows you to hold it gently. Gently stroke the top of his foot and don't grip it too tightly or pull the leg or you'll only cause resentment and resistance.

When he allows you to hold his foot, verbally praise him by saying, "good boy, good boy!" Introduce the procedure slowly, one foot at a time, being patient and gentle, and your dog will be more cooperative.

If the hair on his foot covers his nails, making it difficult for you to see them, wet your thumb and push the hair back to expose the nail (or poke the nails through an old nylon stocking).

Snip off a tiny bit of nail at first. Give your dog a small food treat and praise him by saying, "good boy, good boy!" If your puppy allows you to continue, do so. It's a successful first session if you've clipped just a few of his nails. Cut any remaining nails in several sessions, if necessary.

Get a dog used to grooming when he's young and he will have no trouble accepting it when he's an adult.

When using the nail clippers, hold them according to the directions on the package. At a point just below the bend of the nail, cut each nail at a slight upward angle toward the dog. If the nails ever grow too long, clip them as short as possible just beyond the quick, then trim the tips every other day (which will force the quick to recede) until the nails are the correct length.

Tending to the Ears

The hair inside the Miniature Schnauzer's ears keeps growing and needs to be removed with a tweezers. If not, it will grow downward into the ear canal and can cause infection. If your dog is groomed professionally, be sure the groomer plucks the hair from your dog's ears at each visit. If you groom your dog yourself, you'll need to do it. Any time hair accumulates, it must be removed.

There is a special powder made to make it easier for your thumb and forefinger to grasp and pull out the easily visible hairs inside the ear near the surface. Sprinkle some powder onto the inner surface of the ear (*never* into the ear canal) and fluff it around by gently tapping the ear's surface with your forefinger. Your dog will be manageable if you hold his head gently against your body with your free hand.

Using the tweezers or a hemostat (an invaluable tool), grasp a few strands of hair and withdraw them. Be careful with the hemostat—don't poke the skin or grasp a bit of flesh. Be sure to remove only a few hairs at a time or you will hurt your dog. Continue plucking the hair until it's all gone. Spreading the ear will enable you to see the hair growing deeper inside the ear. If necessary, add more powder.

After the ear is cleared of hair, the powder must be removed or it will accumulate bacteria. Using a cotton ball or a cotton swab dipped into baby lotion (but not dripping with it), gently wipe the inside of the ear.

Whether your dog is groomed professionally or by you, regularly check the ears for any wax or dirt that accumulates. Place three or four drops of a commercial canine ear cleansing solution into the ear and massage the ear at the base for three minutes to distribute the solution. Follow the directions, using cotton balls and plastic gloves if you want. Never use cotton swabs. These can damage the eardrum if pushed in at the wrong angle. With a series of cotton balls, gently cleanse the ear, removing all of the accumulated debris. Then use a clean cotton ball to remove all of the liquid solution.

Coat Care

Your Miniature Schnauzer's coat needs brushing, bathing, clipping, plucking, and scissoring. Your dog should be brushed *at least* two or three times a week—every day is better. If you have a puppy, you can wait until his coat is long enough to brush.

The trick to having a smooth Miniature Schnauzer coat without any knotted hairs or mats is to keep it brushed. If you get rid of the tiny knots before they become huge masses of tangled hair, you'll have less work to do and the job will be less painful to your dog—who otherwise would have to stand there the whole time and lose big chunks of his coat.

Use a slicker brush with wire bristles that bend. With your fingers, remove any burrs or foreign matter from the coat. Separate any mats with your fingers, then use the end teeth of a coarse metal comb to divide the hair into smaller sections and comb out the small areas.

When you brush larger areas, be careful to avoid digging the bristles into the skin. Brush the coat thoroughly from the skin outward, not just on the coat's surface. That's because your dog actually has two coats—a wiry topcoat and a soft undercoat—and you need to get all the way down to the undercoat.

To remove dirt and loose skin particles, brush in the direction the coat grows, then in the opposite direction, and finally again in the direction the hair grows. This pattern stimulates circulation and secretion of the natural skin oils and helps build a healthy coat.

With the furnishings, on each leg, brush downward in the direction the hair grows, starting at the feet, then moving upward to the next layer and the next layer, until the entire leg is brushed. Then brush upward, and again downward.

When you're ready to brush the beard and the mustache, start brushing them at the outer edge and move to the next layer, until you reach the skin. The last step in caring for your Miniature Schnauzer's coat is combing everything with a coarse-toothed metal comb.

An adult Miniature Schnauzer with a clipped coat needs so little maintenance that he can have a spiffy appearance every day of his

Your dog should be brushed several times a week.

life. Daily brushing of four legs, two eyebrows, a beard, and a mustache is a small investment of time for such a great return.

The Clipped Coat

If your take your dog to a professional groomer to have his coat clipped, be sure the groomer understands the breed and is familiar with the attractive haircut pattern that preserves the Miniature Schnauzer's dapper look. Many groomers keep the underside coat between the forelegs and rear legs long, which isn't really how the breed should look. Show the groomer a picture of a Miniature Schnauzer in a show coat. If you want your dog's coat length to taper as it reaches back to the tummy and rear legs, be sure to request that style.

If you decide to do the job yourself and save some money, study the procedure and ask an experienced friend or breeder to demonstrate the technique for you and to teach you how to do it. The clipped coat pattern is relatively easy to learn and simple to do.

The Show Coat

Maintaining your Miniature Schnauzer in a stripped coat is not easy, and it is not likely that a commercial groomer will know the procedure or be willing to

A clipped coat is not all that difficult to do yourself. You'll still need to keep your dog's beard and eyebrows nicely trimmed.

accept the challenge. You will have to learn from an exhibitor, breeder, or professional handler by watching them do it. Ask them to teach you the technique. Not only is it intricate and time consuming, but it must be done in several stages and be precisely timed for each show season.

The stripped show coat shows off the Miniature Schnauzer in his most typically attractive appearance, but the periods between a show coat that has shed out and the next new show coat can be long and unattractive.

Decide in advance if you want to make the commitment to keeping your dog in a show coat and can devote the time and energy it requires.

Preventing Fleas and Ticks

While you're into getting up close and personal with your dog's coat, you'll also want to make sure he doesn't have any fleas or ticks. Fleas and ticks can be your dog's worst enemies. When a Miniature Schnauzer has fleas, he scratches incessantly or bites at his own skin to get rid of them. Soon the dog's hair falls out from the irritation. He will suffer a loss of blood and can contract a serious parasite: tapeworms.

The pests first show up on your dog's thighs and hindquarters and quickly spread to his stomach, lower back, and up to the neck and head. If you see your dog scratching and biting to relieve irritating itching, he may have fleas. Examine his skin by pulling back the hairs. Any small black and white specks are probably flea feces or eggs. If you crush some of the black specks between your fingers and they leave red spots, they're definitely flea feces—digested blood. You may even see the fleas moving quickly through the hair.

Here's good news: There are new products available from your veterinarian that do a great job of preventing fleas and ticks from hitching a free ride on your dog. These products are described in the box on page 74.

If your Miniature Schnauzer has fleas, the only way to get rid of them completely is to treat both your dog and the environment (see the box on pages 76–77). That means the house, the yard, the car, and any area with which your dog has come into contact—everything from carpets to furniture to your bed to the dog's spot outside. It will be necessary to rid every area of not only the fleas, but also the flea eggs, which hatch into a new crop of pests in eight to ten days. Fumigation with a commercial insecticide (a flea fogger) or the services of a professional exterminator may be necessary.

Camping and hiking in the deep woods is not the only way a dog can get fleas and ticks. They also lurk in backyards and parks. Check your dog frequently for these pests during the warm months.

New Products in the Fight Against Fleas

At one time, battling fleas meant exposing your dog and yourself to toxic dips, sprays, powders, and collars. But today there are flea preventives that work very well and are safe for your dog, you, and the environment. The two most common types are insect growth regulators (IGRs), which stop the immature flea from developing or maturing, and adult flea killers. To deal with an active infestation, experts usually recommend a product that has both.

These next-generation flea fighters generally come in one of two forms:

- **Topical treatments or spot-ons.** These products are applied to the skin, usually between the shoulder blades. The product is absorbed through the skin into the dog's system. Among the most widely available spot-ons are Advantage (kills adult fleas and larvae), Revolution (kills adult fleas), Frontline Plus (kills adult fleas and larvae, plus an IGR), K-9 Advantix (kills adult fleas and larvae), and BioSpot (kills adult fleas and larvae, plus an IGR).
- **Systemic products.** This is a pill your dog swallows that transmits a chemical throughout the dog's bloodstream. When a flea bites the dog, it picks up this chemical, which then prevents the flea's eggs from developing. Among the most widely available systemic products are Program (kills larvae only, plus an IGR) and Capstar (kills adult fleas).

Make sure you read all the labels and apply the products exactly as recommended, and that you check to make sure they are safe for puppies.

Treat your dog at the same time you treat the house, car, and yard to avoid reinfestation. There are lots of products available, so ask your veterinarian or the dog's breeder for a recommendation. Young puppies should not be subjected to insecticides, collars, sprays, or other toxic products. And whatever products you use, be sure to follow the instructions on the label and read the precautions before you begin. And do not combine flea-control products, because the cumulative effect can be toxic.

If fleas are a serious problem in your area, discuss a preventive program with your veterinarian.

Ticks

Ticks are small, wingless arachnids (relatives of the spider) that come in many sizes, depending on which part of the country you live in. They live in dense undergrowth, such as woods, fields, and grassy dunes. And they carry diseases, most notably Rocky Mountain spotted fever and Lyme disease.

If you live in a rural area or an area with a heavy deer population, you should check your Miniature Schnauzer's entire body for ticks every day.

Unfortunately, none of the flea-control products are 100 percent effective against a tick grabbing a quick bite. You may have to remove a tick from your dog now and again. The box on page 78 explains how.

Lyme Disease

Since its discovery in Lyme, Connecticut, in the 1970s, Lyme disease has spread to almost the entire United States. It is a virus spread by deer ticks, whose hosts are deer and mice.

When an infected deer tick bites another animal, it passes the disease through its saliva into the blood of the bitten animal. On people, the site of an infected deer tick bite will usually develop a red circle around it. On dogs, this circle could be difficult if not impossible to see.

The best prevention is intervention: Check your outdoor-loving dog every day for these pests, and remove them promptly. Symptoms of Lyme disease include joint stiffness and pain, and lethargy. Your veterinarian can do a blood test to detect for Lyme disease, but if it comes back negative, don't rule Lyme out. Have your dog retested.

Lyme is a serious disease, and you should keep a close eye on your Schnauzer if you know he's been exposed. If it's caught soon enough, treatment with antibiotics usually clears up the symptoms.

Making Your Environment Flea Free

There are many good flea preventives available from your veterinarian that you can safely use. If there are already fleas on your dog, there are fleas in your home, yard, and car, even if you can't see them. Take these steps to combat them.

In your home:

- Wash whatever is washable (the dog bed, sheets, blankets, pillow covers, slipcovers, curtains, etc.).
- Vacuum everything else in your home—furniture, floors, rugs, everything. Pay special attention to the folds and crevices in upholstery, cracks between floorboards, and the spaces between the floor and the baseboards. Flea larvae are sensitive to sunlight, so inside the house they prefer deep carpet, bedding, and cracks and crevices.
- When you're done, throw the vacuum cleaner bag away—in an outside garbage can.
- Use a nontoxic flea-killing powder, such as Flea Busters or Zodiac FleaTrol, to treat your carpets (but remember, it does not control fleas elsewhere in the house). The powder stays deep in the carpet and kills fleas (using a form of boric acid) for up to a year.
- If you have a particularly serious flea problem, consider using a fogger or long-lasting spray to kill any adult and larval fleas, or having a professional exterminator treat your home.

The Bath

Always brush your dog before you bathe him. If you wait until after the bath, your dog's coat will have wet knots that are very difficult to comb out.

To your Miniature Schnauzer, bath time should be fun time. Set aside enough time to bathe your dog so that you're not rushed and can enjoy the experience. If you have fun, your dog will have fun. Gather all of the bathing accessories you'll need ahead of time, including the towels, cotton balls, shampoo, conditioner, and a hair dryer. Nothing is more annoying than having a wet dog without a towel.

Don't plan on wearing your best clothes when you're bathing your dog. Wear something that you don't mind getting wet. No matter how well trained your

In your car:

- Take out the floor mats and hose them down with a strong stream of water, then hang them up to dry in the sun.
- Wash any towels, blankets, or other bedding you regularly keep in the car.
- Thoroughly vacuum the entire interior of your car, paying special attention to the seams between the bottom and back of the seats.
- When you're done, throw the vacuum cleaner bag away—in an outside garbage can.

In your yard:

- Flea larvae prefer shaded areas that have plenty of organic material and moisture, so rake the yard thoroughly and bag all the debris in tightly sealed bags.
- Spray your yard with an insecticide that has residual activity for at least thirty days. Insecticides that use a form of boric acid are nontoxic. Some newer products contain an insect growth regulator (such as fenoxycarb) and need to be applied only once or twice a year.
- For an especially difficult flea problem, consider having an exterminator treat your yard.
- Keep your yard free of piles of leaves, weeds, and other organic debris. Be especially careful in shady, moist areas, such as under bushes.

dog is in the tub, he may try to shake the water off and in the process you'll get a little wet. OK, maybe a lot wet!

When you're ready, test the water temperature with the inside of your wrist to make sure the water isn't too hot or too cold before putting your Miniature Schnauzer in the tub. Since some dogs just don't like water, once your dog hears the bath water running, he may run the other way. Be prepared to lure him into the bathroom with a small food treat.

Once he's in the tub, wet your Miniature Schnauzer thoroughly before adding any shampoo. Put cotton balls inside your dog's ears to keep the water from getting in, which could cause infection. When your Miniature Schnauzer is thoroughly wet, lather up the shampoo on his back and briskly rub his coat.

How to Get Rid of a Tick

Although Frontline, K-9 Advantix, and BioSpot, the new generation of flea and tick fighters, are partially effective in killing ticks once they are on your dog, they are not 100 percent effective and will not keep ticks from biting your dog in the first place. During tick season (which, depending on where you live, can be spring, summer, and/or fall), examine your dog every day for ticks. Pay particular attention to your dog's neck, behind the ears, the armpits, and the groin.

When you find a tick, use a pair of tweezers to grasp the tick as close as possible to the dog's skin and pull it out using firm, steady pressure. Check to make sure you get the whole tick (mouth parts left in your dog's skin can cause an infection), then dab the wound with a little hydrogen peroxide and some antibiotic ointment. Watch for signs of inflammation.

Ticks carry very serious diseases that are transmittable to humans, so dispose of the tick safely. *Never* crush it between your fingers. Don't flush it down the toilet either, because the tick will survive the trip and infect another animal. Instead, use the tweezers to place the tick in a tight-sealing jar or plastic dish with a little alcohol, put on the lid and dispose of the container in an outdoor garbage can. Wash the tweezers thoroughly with hot water and alcohol.

Shampoo his head, legs, chest, tummy, and rear. Remove the cotton from his ears and, without any shampoo, use a clean, damp, wrung-out washcloth to wipe out the inside of the ears. Replace fresh cotton in each ear to dry it out.

Thoroughly rinse your dog's body with warm, not hot, water until there's no trace of shampoo remaining in his coat. Then rinse again! Try not to get any soapy water in your dog's eyes and ears.

Use the conditioner to remove any tangles and be sure to rinse a second time. If your dog is really dirty, bathe and rinse him again.

Be sure to rinse your dog thoroughly after his shampoo. When you think you have all the shampoo out, rinse again.

Squeeze the excess water from your dog's beard and eyebrows and wrap a towel around him to absorb as much moisture as possible. Use another towel to dry him or use a hair dryer on a low setting until the coat is barely damp. A special canine hair dryer on a stand will enable you to get the job done hands-free in no time. Do not let your dog go anyplace that is chilly or drafty until he is completely dry.

The last step is brushing and combing your dog's coat to make sure there are no mats or tangles.

Chapter 8

Keeping Your Miniature Schnauzer Safe and Healthy

Some dogs live their lives without any illnesses, while others have more than their share. As a rule, Miniature Schnauzers are a pretty healthy breed. But, like any breed of dog, they can get sick or hurt. It's a good idea to know what can make your dog sick. That way you can be on the lookout for any early warning signs or take steps to prevent the problem through genetic testing, dietary management, or medication.

Inherited Diseases

Like people, Miniature Schnauzers can inherit diseases from their relatives when defective genes are passed from generation to generation. Although no one has a crystal ball to predict if a puppy will have a genetic weakness when she grows up, it does help to know what diseases Miniature Schnauzers may be prone to having. Some (but not all) defects can be tested for in advance, and conscientious breeders will not breed dogs who carry defective genes that can be passed on to their puppies. The following are the most common defects that afflict Miniature Schnauzers (among other breeds). Be sure to ask your dog's breeder if any of these abnormalities have shown up in his or her dogs.

Progressive Retinal Atrophy

Progressive retinal atrophy (PRA) is an inherited eye disease in which the cells of the retina gradually degenerate, leading to loss of sight. Initially, your dog will lose night vision, and eventually she'll go blind. PRA affects Miniature Schnauzers and many other breeds. Interestingly, the severity of PRA affects different breeds at different ages, causing some to lose their sight within months, and others, years.

PRA is expressed in a pattern unique to the Miniature Schnauzer. One form affects puppies, who lose their sight between 8 and 12 months of age. Another form affects adults, who become blind at around 3 years of age.

While the disease itself cannot be cured, its elimination in a breed may be possible through widespread testing and careful breeding. PRA-affected dogs obviously must not be bred. Unaffected dogs (those with normal eyes) who carry the gene may be bred, but only to other dogs who do not carry the gene for PRA, since half their offspring would inherit the defective gene. Two carriers also should not be bred.

Researchers have identified the gene responsible for one of the two or possibly more forms of PRA that occur in Miniature Schnauzers. To determine the presence or absence of the disease in a dog, her eyes must be examined annually by a board-certified veterinary ophthalmologist, who sends the test findings to the Canine Eye Registration Foundation (CERF), where the results of each breed's eye tests are analyzed. Annual eye tests are necessary because a dog's early tests may find her to be unaffected, but a later test may show the disease.

Cataracts

Cataracts are as common in older dogs as they are in older humans. The lens becomes opaque and interferes with vision. A veterinary ophthalmologist evaluates a dog's eyes and surgically removes the cataracts. Besides affecting senior Miniature Schnauzers, congenital cataracts can be present in newborn pups. These can be detected as soon as their eyes are open with a relatively simple and inexpensive examination using a slit lamp.

According to the American Miniature Schnauzer web site, the club has been working to eliminate congenital cataracts by asking its members to have dogs used for breeding, and all puppies, examined by a veterinary ophthalmologist. The club has also asked members to spay or neuter any dog who has congenital cataracts or who has produced any affected puppies.

Because of this national breed club effort, congenital cataracts have become very rare among Miniature Schnauzers being shown in the United States and Canada.

Breeders can test for some inherited eye diseases to avoid breeding affected puppies.

Mycobacterium Avium Infection

While researchers cannot verify that *Mycobacterium avium* infection is genetic, Miniature Schnauzers are highly susceptible to this canine form of tuberculosis. There is no vaccine available to protect a dog against it, and it is deadly. Researchers are hoping to develop a genetic test to identify the carriers of this disease.

Portosystemic Shunt

In a dog with a portosystemic shunt (also known as a liver shunt or a portosystemic vascular anomaly), blood is diverted around the liver into the bloodstream without being detoxified. Many cases are diagnosed in young animals, but a Mini Schnauzer may develop a liver shunt later in life as a result of any serious liver disease.

Listlessness, walking or running in circles, drinking excessive amounts of water, frequent urination, and lack of muscular coordination are a few of the symptoms. Your veterinarian can test for the presence of this disorder and provide a special diet. The defect can be surgically corrected; without surgery, severely affected animals probably will die of liver failure.

Pancreatitis

An inflammation of the pancreas, this condition affects Miniature Schnauzers who are obese. Eating large quantities of high-fat food may be the cause. Symptoms include depression, loss of appetite, and vomiting. Treatment for severe cases includes withholding food and giving intravenous fluid therapy, while mild cases will abate on their own. To prevent future flare-ups, veterinarians recommend not feeding your dog high-fat meals.

Urinary Stones

According to the databases of both the University of Minnesota and the University of California at Davis, Miniature Schnauzers are one of the top four small breeds at risk for forming urinary tract stones.

They form three types of stones: struvite (due to urinary tract infections), calcium oxalate (more common in middle-aged to older dogs), and urate (more common in puppies and young adults with a portal vascular anomaly). Dogs with stones may be treated nonsurgically. With successful treatment and a change in diet, they can live a normal, healthy life.

Myotonia Congenita

Mini Schnauzer puppies show signs of this skeletal muscle disorder when they are just a few weeks old. Dogs will have a hard time getting up from a sleeping position, will bunny hop when running, or will have a stiff gait. Other signs include difficulty swallowing and an enlarged tongue that stiffens when you touch it. Although treatment can alleviate some of the symptoms, dogs will never be able to eat or exercise normally.

There is a DNA screening test that detects the disorder in carriers and confirms a diagnosis in affected dogs.

Cushing's Disease

A relatively common hormonal disease, Cushing's is caused from the overproduction of cortisol by the adrenal glands. A few signs include excessive appetite, hematomas (localized pockets of collected blood), changes in coat color, scaling, and wounds healing slowly. Medication is available to improve the quality of life.

Autoimmune Disease

More and more dogs of all breeds are being diagnosed with autoimmune disease, but Miniature Schnauzers are particularly at risk. A few of the typical signs

Vaccines

What vaccines dogs need and how often they need them has been a subject of controversy for several years. Researchers, health care professionals, vaccine manufacturers, and dog owners do not always agree on which vaccines each dog needs or how often booster shots must be given.

In 2003, the American Animal Hospital Association released vaccination guidelines and recommendations that have helped dog owners and veterinarians sort through much of the controversy and conflicting information. The guidelines designate four vaccines as core, or essential, because of the serious nature of the diseases and their widespread distribution. These are canine distemper virus, canine parvovirus, canine adenovirus-2, and rabies. The general recommendations for their use (except rabies, for which you must follow local laws) are:

- Vaccinate puppies at 6–8 weeks, 9–11 weeks, and 12–14 weeks.
- Give a booster shot when the dog is 1 year old.

are stiffness, sore joints, abdominal tenderness, jaundice, and susceptibility to infections.

Repeated combination vaccines in young puppies may be the cause of this problem, which can cause chronic debilitating diseases later in life.

Von Willebrand's Disease

Mini Schnauzers and several other breeds suffer from Von Willebrand's Disease (VWD). Like hemophilia, dogs with VWD are deficient in factor that causes blood to clot. The symptoms include nosebleeds, intermittent lameness caused by bleeding into joints, and hematomas.

- Give a subsequent booster shot every three years, unless there are risk factors that make it necessary to vaccinate more or less often.

Noncore vaccines should only be considered for those dogs who risk exposure to a particular disease because of geographic area, lifestyle, frequency of travel, or other issues. They include vaccines against distemper-measles virus, canine parainfluenza virus, leptospirosis, Bordetella bronchiseptica, and Borrelia burgdorferi (Lyme disease).

Vaccines that are not generally recommended because the disease poses little risk to dogs or is easily treatable, or the vaccine has not been proven to be effective, are those against Giardia, canine coronavirus, and canine adenovirus-1.

Often, combination injections are given to puppies, with one shot containing several core and noncore vaccines. Your veterinarian may be reluctant to use separate shots that do not include the noncore vaccines, because they must be specially ordered. If you are concerned about these noncore vaccines, talk to your vet.

Schnauzer Bumps

Many Miniature Schnauzers have small wartlike nodes on their skin. These are known as Schnauzer bumps. Schnauzer bumps do not exude fluid; they simply exist and typically bother the dog's owner far more than the dog. Actually, they do not bother the dog at all.

Much has been written about why they crop up and what to do about them, and opinions on the subject vary. Perhaps some day the mystery will be solved.

Schnauzer bumps do not secrete fatty, oily substances. If you see these types of secretions, your dog needs medical attention.

Just because a genetic problem exists in a breed, it does not mean every dog of that breed will inherit the problem. Each dog inherits a unique combination of genes from both parents.

Internal Parasites

The internal parasites that affect your Miniature Schnauzer include a variety of worms and protozoa. They make no useful contribution, and, undetected, they can rob your dog of blood, food, energy, and, possibly, life. If your puppy or dog is acting listless, won't eat, coughs a lot without coughing anything up, seems to have a bloated belly, or if you notice white slivers in her stools, she may have worms.

For all of these parasites, talk to your veterinarian about regularly testing your dog's stool. If you see any signs of worms, take a fresh stool sample (and your dog!) to the vet as soon as possible so she can be treated. Over-the-counter worming medications are not as effective as those prescribed by your vet, because there are many different types of worms and not all preparations kill every type.

Hookworms

These worms have hooklike mouth parts by which they attach themselves to the lining of the intestines. They commonly occur in puppies, but adults also may be infested. They are contracted when the dog swallows the parasite's larvae or when the larvae penetrate the dog's skin. They are visible only under a microscope.

A mildly infected dog has diarrhea, loses weight, and has a poor coat. A heavily infested dog becomes weak and anemic from blood loss. The condition is treatable, but infection can be avoided by keeping the dog's environment sanitary. Remove feces frequently, keep the lawn short and relatively dry, and wash down paved areas with disinfectants.

Roundworms

These are very common in puppies, and adult dogs acquire them by licking contaminated ground or eating smaller animals that carry roundworm larvae. Affected puppies are weak and thin with potbellies; have dull, dry coats; have diarrhea; and cough and vomit.

Roundworms look like white, firm pieces of thin spaghetti about one to three inches long, and often coil like springs. Adult dogs who become infested may show no signs of infection. The condition is treatable, and the sanitary program described for preventing hookworms is recommended. Roundworms can be passed to children, in whom serious diseases can result.

Tapeworms

Rare in puppies, tapeworms more frequently infest mature dogs who have eaten an infected host—a piece of meat, an animal, or an insect (a flea, louse, or mosquito). The head of the worm attaches to the intestinal lining and produces egg-filled body segments, which eventually break off and are excreted.

The detached segments may be seen in the hair around the dog's anus, in her bedding, or in the stool. When alive, the segments are off-white and flat and wave back and forth or crawl; when dried out, they may become yellow, translucent, and look like grains of uncooked rice. Symptoms may be weight loss and diarrhea.

Whipworms

These worms are thin, white, shaped like a whip, less than an inch long, and difficult to see. They inhabit the dog's lower intestinal tract. Some infected dogs have no symptoms, while others will have intermittent watery diarrhea, anemia, weight loss, weakness, and a generally poor appearance. Because licking or sniffing contaminated ground can infest dogs, a dry and sanitary environment should be maintained.

Internal parasites are a much more serious problem for little puppies than they are for adult dogs.

Heartworms

Heartworms enter your dog's bloodstream via the bite of an infected mosquito. They mature in your dog's heart, reaching a length of five to twelve inches, and present a very serious, life-threatening risk. An infected dog will tire easily, have a chronic cough, and lose weight. While an infected dog may be treated with drugs to destroy the adult worms, it is far simpler and safer to protect your dog with preventive medicine. The preventive must be taken throughout mosquito season (which may be year-round in warm climates).

Every year, before putting your dog on the preventive, your veterinarian will test for the presence of heartworms in your Mini Schnauzer's blood. The test must be negative before the preventive is started, because the medicine that prevents an infestation can complicate matters if your dog is already affected.

Giardia

Giardia is a protozoan, and it infects animals who drink contaminated water. Giardia is a common parasite of wild animals, so any water source from which wild animals drink can be infected. And if your Mini Schnauzer also drinks that water, he can get infected from it. That's why it's a good idea to bring water from home when you go on a trip with your dog, especially if you will be walking, hiking, or camping.

Diarrhea is a symptom of a giardia infection, so if your dog develops diarrhea shortly after you've been camping, for example, you can suspect she's been infected. Make sure to tell your veterinarian you suspect giardia.

Common Problems

Because Miniature Schnauzers require frequent and specialized grooming, you're in a good position to spot a health problem early on before it progresses. Here are some things to look for.

Ear Problems

By regularly checking and cleaning your dog's ear canals, you'll be able to distinguish a healthy ear from an infected one. A dog's ear canals are normally light pink, they have a slight collection of wax, and there's no odor.

Your Miniature Schnauzer needs veterinary care if the inside of the ear is swollen or tender, has a foul odor, has a profuse collection of wax, if a sloshing noise is heard when she shakes her head, or if the inside skin color is red. These could all be signs of an inner ear infection, probably caused by yeast, bacteria, or ear mites. Yeast and bacteria grow rapidly in dark, damp areas, which is why the inner ear is an ideal spot for them.

You can prevent ear infections by cleaning your dog's ears regularly, as described in chapter 7. Cropped and uncropped ears have the same likelihood of getting an ear infection.

Any ear problem will get worse if it is not treated. If your veterinarian recommends ointment or ear drops, place the medication into the ear and vigorously massage the area just below the canal to channel the medication deeply into the ear.

Ear Mites

Ear mites live and feed in the dog's ear canals, causing her to vigorously shake her head and scratch her ears, visibly demonstrating her extreme

Check your dog's ears regularly. They should look and smell clean.

discomfort. They can also cause a brown, waxy discharge. They are microscopic, so your veterinarian must make a definitive diagnosis. Your vet will also need to treat the ears initially to flush them out. Your veterinarian can then teach you how to clean and treat the problem at home with medication formulated to eliminate ear mites.

Skin Problems

Healthy skin is smooth and flexible with no visible scales, scabs, growths, or red areas. It is free of dandruff, is not excessively oily, and has no bald areas (except during the stages of stripping a coat, which is a special grooming technique).

To prevent your dog from making any skin problem worse by biting an itch or licking a wound, saturate a cloth with mouthwash, place it on the spot, and rub it gently through the coat to reach the skin. Dogs hate the taste, and the product contains nothing harmful.

Seborrhea

This results from an abnormal production of skin oils, causing a flaky, scaly skin or greasy, yellow-brown scales. A dog suffering from seborrhea will often have a rancid smell. Seborrhea in Miniature Schnauzers is sometimes incurable, but may be kept under control with a special medicated shampoo.

Hot Spots

These are skin infections that appear as patches of red, irritated skin with hair loss. The spots seem to form overnight, and are caused by the dog constantly licking or scratching at the infected spot. Hot spots can be difficult to treat, because unless the dog stops licking at the spot, it won't heal. Hot spots need to be treated with antibiotic ointment, and your dog must be prevented from licking and picking at them. Discuss options with your veterinarian.

Allergies

Just like people, dogs have or acquire allergies to all sorts of things. Sources of allergies include dust, insect bites, carpet fibers, a new shampoo, a disagreeable inhalant, and even types of food.

What is an allergy? It is a reaction to the irritating substance, called an allergen. When the allergen comes into contact with skin or is breathed in, a complex set of events causes the body to react against it. If the allergen affects the eyes, they will tear and possibly swell; if the allergen affects the nose or respiratory system, there will be a thick discharge, like sniffles or sneezing; if the skin is

Just like people, dogs can be allergic to all sorts of things.

affected, it gets itchy, red, inflamed, and even bumpy. The hair could fall out. While allergies most often affect the respiratory system of people, they most often affect the skin of dogs.

The most common canine allergy is *flea allergy dermatitis,* which is an allergy to flea bites. Affected dogs itch all the time and get red, raw spots that may eventually cease to grow hair and become scaly and thick. Dogs with flea allergies need extra attention paid to their skin and environment to keep them flea-free. See chapter 7 for more on preventing fleas.

Your veterinarian can try to determine what it is your dog is allergic to, so you can remove that substance from your home and anywhere your dog may go. Sometimes it's as simple as changing food, washing with a new detergent, or getting a different kind of dog bedding. Allergies are typically treated with cortisone, which can have side effects, so make sure your veterinarian explains what your dog is being treated with and what you can expect.

External Parasites

Fleas and ticks have already been discussed in chapter 7, and ear mites were covered on pages 89–90. But there are other creepy crawlies that can torment your Miniature Schnauzer.

Scabies

This is a condition that spreads rapidly between dogs; it also affects humans. The microscopic mite burrows beneath the dog's skin, causing intense itching and loss of hair, particularly on the ears, elbows, legs, and face. If untreated, the dog's entire body will develop *sarcoptic mange*. Scrapings from the dog's skin, examined by the veterinarian under a microscope, will confirm their presence, and an intense treatment of insecticide and medication will relieve the itching until the mites are eradicated.

Demodectic Mange

This develops from a microscopic mite who lives in the hair follicles, causing thick, red skin, hair loss, and the eventual formation of pustules in infected hair follicles. The mites, diagnosed by a veterinarian's microscopic examination of skin scrapings and hair roots, can be treated with an insecticide, but the cure is more effective before the pustules are allowed to form.

Eye Problems

Your dog's eyes should be bright, shiny, and free from excessive tearing or discharge. The conjunctiva (the moist pink inner lining of the eyelids) should not be swollen, inflamed, or have a yellow discharge. If any of these conditions are noted, there are many possible causes.

Possibilities include an allergic reaction, an injury, a foreign body in the eye, an irritant, or a disease whose source is parasitic—all of which require prompt veterinary attention.

Mouth and Throat Problems

If something's affecting your dog's mouth, you'll notice by her actions. She will drool excessively, paw at her mouth, shake her head, cough or gag, have bad breath, have a bloody discharge from her mouth, and lose her appetite (perhaps due to her inability to chew or swallow).

The first thing to do is check to see if something is lodged in her mouth, such as a stone or a piece of wood. Foreign bodies may be anything from slivers of wood (from chewed sticks, twigs, or furniture legs) to fabric, plastic, or whatever material her mischief has led her to. The object may be wedged between her teeth or across the roof of her mouth. It happens!

When your veterinarian has removed the object, the dog's breathing will have a scratchy sound. Get a specific assessment from your veterinarian, who will probably prescribe antibiotics and a soft, bland diet. Be sure to treat the injured area to avoid infection.

A foreign body in your dog's windpipe is indicated by a sudden, intense fit of coughing after she has vomited or following her inhalation of foreign matter. If your dog is choking, you may need to give her an abdominal thrust or the Heimlich maneuver to remove it.

Other problems include *glossitis,* an inflammation of the tongue. This condition causes the edges of the tongue to look red and swollen. Common causes are excessive tartar on the teeth, foreign bodies, cuts, burns, insect stings, and an association with other diseases. Your dog will refuse to eat, will drool, and her tongue may bleed or exude a thick, brown, smelly discharge.

Your dog's breath should smell clean and fresh. If it doesn't, take her to see the veterinarian.

A sore throat *(pharyngitis)* is fairly common in dogs, causing them to cough and gag, lose appetite, and possibly run a fever. As with people, the throat will appear red and inflamed. Veterinary treatment is needed.

Respiratory Problems

If a dog has respiratory problems, there's a nasal discharge, sneezing, coughing, noisy or difficult breathing, and abnormal sounds within the chest.

Kennel Cough

Kennel cough, while not life threatening, is readily spread from one dog to another and is caused by several viruses and by *Bordatella bronchiseptica* (a bacteria). The dog will have a dry, hacking cough, and may have a nasal discharge. The dog should be kept in a warm, humid environment, isolated from other dogs. The veterinarian will administer antibiotics.

A vaccine has been developed to prevent kennel cough, and most reputable boarding kennels and canine training classes require a dog to be inoculated before she is admitted.

Bronchitis

This is a respiratory infection that often follows a bout of kennel cough. Your dog's dry, rough cough will usually last for days or weeks, and she may retch following a coughing spell, sometimes bringing up foamy saliva. Antibiotics must be administered.

Urogenital Problems

Male and female dogs are susceptible to a number of diseases of their reproductive organs, such as infections of the uterus, prostate diseases, and various cancers. The best way to treat these is to prevent them from occurring. This is easily and humanely done by spaying your female Mini Schnauzer or neutering your male.

It's normal for a mature male dog to discharge a small amount of white or yellowish material from the prepuce (the skin covering the penis). Suspect infection if he frequently licks the prepuce, if the discharge is excessive, discolored, or foul smelling, or if the penis is extremely red with small bumps on it and the lining of the prepuce. The irritating infection is treatable by the veterinarian.

The Anal Region

On either side of the anus is a gland that secretes a thick, liquid lubricant that enables the dog to mark territory. If the glands, known as the anal sacs, become clogged, your dog will lick the anus and drag her rear on the ground. To relieve the discomfort, the anal sacs will need to be emptied, a procedure you can do at home. If you find it too distasteful, inform your veterinarian so he or she can do it regularly.

To express the anal sacs, hold the tail up firmly with one hand. With a piece of gauze or tissue in the other hand, encircle the anal area with your thumb and forefinger at the eight and four o'clock positions, respectively, then push in and squeeze.

The anal sac material, which has a vile odor, should exude from the two gland ducts on the anus, which you can then wipe away. The procedure should be repeated when the glandular material accumulates, or at regular intervals to avoid the accumulation. If the process, when needed, is neglected, the glands become infected (evidenced by bloody or puslike discharge) and will require veterinary care.

Loss of Appetite

When your dog loses interest in her food, something is wrong. Refusing to eat can be a sign of several different illnesses. The dog may just have an upset tummy. Or the food could be spoiled. If she's not acting her usual bouncy self, take her to the veterinarian.

Why Spay and Neuter?

Breeding dogs is a serious undertaking that should only be part of a well-planned breeding program. Why? Because dogs pass on their physical and behavioral problems to their offspring. Even healthy, well-behaved dogs can pass on problems in their genes.

Is your dog so sweet that you'd like to have a litter of puppies just like her? If you breed her to another dog, the pups will not have the same genetic heritage she has. Breeding her *parents* again will increase the odds of a similar pup, but even then, the puppies in the second litter could inherit different genes. In fact, *there is no way to breed a dog to be just like another dog.*

Meanwhile, thousands and thousands of dogs are killed in animal shelters every year simply because they have no homes. Casual breeding is a big contributor to this problem.

If you don't plan to breed your dog, is it still a good idea to spay her or neuter him? Yes!

When you spay your female:

- You avoid her heat cycles, during which she discharges blood and scent.
- It greatly reduces the risk of mammary cancer and eliminates the risk of pyometra (an often fatal infection of the uterus) and uterine cancer.
- It prevents unwanted pregnancies.
- It reduces dominance behaviors and aggression.

When you neuter your male:

- It curbs the desire to roam and to fight with other males.
- It greatly reduces the risk of prostate cancer and eliminates the risk of testicular cancer.
- It helps reduce leg lifting and mounting behavior.
- It reduces dominance behaviors and aggression.

Just like human athletes, canine athletes can get sprains and strains.

If she's normal otherwise, give her the regular food. If she refuses to eat, pick the food up after 20 minutes and dispose of it. Don't give her anything to eat until the next regular meal. Then give her a fresh bowl of the same food. If she still refuses to eat, try giving her another brand of dog food. If she eats it, she may not be sick. Feel free to contact your veterinarian if you are concerned.

Lameness

A dog will limp and be lame when her limbs are painful or weak. The causes include trauma, nutritional imbalance, congenital defects, infection, and Lyme disease. The veterinarian's palpation or X-rays of the affected area should be able to locate the source of the limp. A mild injury may heal by itself in a short time, but a more serious problem will need prompt veterinary attention. A serious problem would be a sprain, fracture, dislocation, or bone disease.

Vomiting

Vomiting is a sign of other problems. A dog who vomits once or twice presents little cause for concern. It may simply be her way of clearing her throat. Most often, she will vomit after eating something irritating to the stomach such as garbage, grass, paper, or any indigestible item.

If she vomits her food and later brings up a frothy, clear or yellow liquid, do not feed her for the next twelve to twenty-four hours, and offer her ice cubes instead of water. Then feed her a bland diet of soft-boiled eggs, cottage cheese, meat baby food, or boiled rice and boiled hamburger with the fat removed. Give small portions on the first day, continuing with the ice cubes.

Once the vomiting has stopped, feed bland foods the next day in normal portions, then return to the dog's regular diet. If the vomiting returns, you should take her to see your veterinarian.

Your veterinarian should also check your dog immediately if vomiting persists; is frequent or forceful; contains blood, fecal matter, worms, or foreign objects; or is accompanied by other signs of illness, such as diarrhea, lethargy, weight loss, or dull coat.

Diarrhea

Loose, soft, and often abundant stools indicate diarrhea, another common sign of trouble in dogs. A mild case is treatable at home if it is not associated with other problems. Causes may be eating irritating or indigestible material, changes or upsets in the dog's normal routine, a sudden change in diet, a switch to unfamiliar water, or the dog's inability to tolerate certain foods. To treat diarrhea at home, do not feed the dog for twenty-four hours, restricting her to ice cubes.

The next day, offer small amounts of the bland food described above to treat vomiting. Continue the diet for three more days, even if the condition improves, then return the dog to her normal diet.

If you see any sudden change in your dog's behavior or activity level, talk to your veterinarian.

When to Call the Veterinarian

Go to the vet right away or take your dog to an emergency veterinary clinic if:

- Your dog is choking.
- Your dog is having trouble breathing.
- Your dog has been injured and you cannot stop the bleeding within a few minutes.
- Your dog has been stung or bitten by an insect and the site is swelling.
- Your dog has several raised areas on his body and more are appearing.
- Your dog is panting excessively, wheezing, unable to catch her breath, breathing heavily or sounds strange when she breathes.
- Your dog is writhing or thrashing his body on the ground without stopping.
- Your dog has been bitten by a snake.
- Your dog has been bitten by another animal (including a dog) and shows any swelling or bleeding.
- Your dog has touched, licked, or in any way been exposed to a poison.
- Your dog has been burned by either heat or caustic chemicals.
- Your dog has been hit by a car.
- Your dog has any obvious broken bones or cannot move or put any weight on one of her limbs without crying or whimpering.
- Your dog has ingested human medication and is acting strangely.
- Your dog has a seizure.

She should see the veterinarian immediately if diarrhea persists for more than twenty-four hours, contains blood, or is accompanied by vomiting, fever, or other signs of distress. Bring a specimen of the stool for your veterinarian to examine.

Constipation

This is the opposite of diarrhea. The stools become so hard and dry that it's difficult if not impossible for the dog to pass them. Constipation can be caused by dehydration, parasites, a poor diet, stress, ingesting a foreign object, or kidney disease. If the problem doesn't go away when you give your dog a mild laxative, more water, and a more fibrous diet, your veterinarian will have to determine the cause.

Make an appointment to see the vet as soon as possible if:

- Your dog has been bitten by a cat, another dog, or a wild animal.
- Your dog has been injured and is still limping an hour later.
- Your dog has unexplained swelling or redness.
- Your dog's appetite changes.
- Your dog vomits repeatedly and can't seem to keep food down, or drools excessively while eating.
- You see any changes in your dog's urination or defecation (pain during elimination, change in regular habits, blood in urine or stool, diarrhea, foul-smelling stool).
- Your dog scoots her rear end on the floor.
- Your dog's energy level, attitude, or behavior changes for no apparent reason.
- Your dog has crusty or cloudy eyes, or excessive tearing or discharge.
- Your dog's nose is dry or chapped, hot, crusty, or runny.
- Your dog's ears smell foul, have a dark discharge, or seem excessively waxy.
- Your dog's gums are inflamed or bleeding, her teeth look brown, or her breath is foul.
- Your dog's skin is red, flaky, itchy, or inflamed, or she keeps chewing at certain spots.
- Your dog's coat is dull, dry, brittle, or bare in spots.
- Your dog's paws are red, swollen, tender, cracked, or the nails are split or too long.

Poisoning

Your Miniature Schnauzer can be poisoned by any number of things, from bad food (garbage) to household cleaners. Keep the numbers of your veterinarian and the ASPCA Animal Poison Control Center near your telephone. Either should be contacted before administering first aid for poisoning.

If the poison can be identified, and the label on its container can be read, the veterinarian can analyze the product contents. Poisons fall into a few basic classes, and each is treated somewhat differently. Basically, treatment is to neutralize the poison and/or to eliminate it from the dog (by coating the dog's stomach with something else or inducing vomiting).

How to Make a Canine First-Aid Kit

If your dog hurts herself, even a minor cut, it can be very upsetting for both of you. Having a first-aid kit handy will help you to help her, calmly and efficiently. What should be in your canine first-aid kit?

- Antibiotic ointment
- Antiseptic and antibacterial cleansing wipes
- Benadryl
- Cotton-tipped applicators
- Disposable razor
- Elastic wrap bandages
- Extra leash and collar
- First-aid book for dogs
- First-aid tape of various widths
- Gauze bandage roll
- Gauze pads of different sizes, including eye pads
- Hydrogen peroxide
- Instant cold compress
- Kaopectate tablets or liquid
- Latex gloves
- Lubricating jelly
- Muzzle
- Nail clippers
- Pen, pencil, and paper for notes and directions
- Pepto-Bismol
- Round-ended scissors and pointy scissors
- Safety pins
- Sterile saline eyewash
- Thermometer (rectal)
- Tweezers

Insecticides and parasite medication are the most common types of intoxications seen in dogs. Signs of toxicosis include muscle trembling, weakness, increased salivation, vomiting, and loss of bowel control, and the signs may vary depending on how badly poisoned the animal is. If these medications had been applied or administered to the dog as a treatment, it is possible that the poisoning resulted from overzealous use (such as using a flea or tick preparation in combination with oral deworming medications).

ASPCA Animal Poison Control Center

The ASPCA Animal Poison Control Center has a staff of licensed veterinarians and board-certified toxicologists available 24 hours a day, 365 days a year. The number to call is (888) 426-4435. You will be charged a consultation fee of $50 per case, charged to most major credit cards. There is no charge for follow-up calls in critical cases. At your request, they will also contact your veterinarian. Specific treatment and information can be provided via fax. Put the number in large, legible print with your other emergency telephone numbers. Be prepared to give your name, address, and phone number; what your dog has gotten into (the amount and how long ago); your dog's breed, age, sex, and weight; and what signs and symptoms the dog is showing. You can log onto www.aspca.org and click on "Animal Poison Control Center" for more information, including a list of toxic and nontoxic plants.

Oral rodenticides, such as rat poison, are usually based on a blood anticlotting factor that reacts rather slowly. Serious toxicity may be averted if the dog is induced to vomit within thirty minutes after ingestion. Some rodenticides (such as gopher poison) that have a strychnine base are acutely toxic, are rapidly absorbed into the dog's system, and can cause convulsions and death in a short period of time.

Acids, alkalis, and petroleum products cause special problems if ingested. Do not induce vomiting. Consult your veterinarian about specific treatment for the particular type of chemical to which the dog has been exposed. If you can't reach your vet, call the ASPCA Animal Poison Control Center.

Antifreeze is very toxic to dogs, and they're very attracted to it because it tastes so sweet. Antifreeze can cause severe kidney damage if even a very small quantity is ingested—such as might be licked from the garage floor. There are dog-safe antifreezes on the market.

Part III

Enjoying Your Miniature Schnauzer

Chapter 9

Training Your Miniature Schnauzer

by Peggy Moran

Training makes your best friend better! A properly trained dog has a happier life and a longer life expectancy. He is also more appreciated by the people he encounters each day, both at home and out and about.

A trained dog walks nicely and joins his family often, going places untrained dogs cannot go. He is never rude or unruly, and he always happily comes when called. When he meets people for the first time, he greets them by sitting and waiting to be petted, rather than jumping up. At home he doesn't compete with his human family, and alone he is not destructive or overly anxious. He isn't continually nagged with words like "no," since he has learned not to misbehave in the first place. He is never shamed, harshly punished, or treated unkindly, and he is a well-loved, involved member of the family.

Sounds good, doesn't it? If you are willing to invest some time, thought, and patience, the words above could soon be used to describe your dog (though perhaps changing "he" to "she"). Educating your pet in a positive way is fun and easy, and there is no better gift you can give your pet than the guarantee of improved understanding and a great relationship.

This chapter will explain how to offer kind leadership, reshape your pet's behavior in a positive and practical way, and even get a head start on simple obedience training.

Understanding Builds the Bond

Dog training is a learning adventure on both ends of the leash. Before attempting to teach their dog new behaviors or change unwanted ones, thoughtful dog owners take the time to understand why their pets behave the way they do, and how their own behavior can be either a positive or negative influence on their dog.

Canine Nature

Loving dogs as much as we do, it's easy to forget they are a completely different species. Despite sharing our homes and living as appreciated members of our families, dogs do not think or learn exactly the same way people do. Even if you love your dog like a child, you must remember to respect the fact that he is actually a dog.

Dogs have no idea when their behavior is inappropriate from a human perspective. They are not aware of the value of possessions they chew or of messes they make or the worry they sometimes seem to cause. While people tend to look at behavior as good and bad or right and wrong, dogs just discover what works and what doesn't work. Then they behave accordingly, learning from their own experiences and increasing or reducing behaviors to improve results for themselves.

You might wonder, "But don't dogs want to please us"? My answer is yes, provided your pleasure reflects back to them in positive ways they can feel and appreciate. Dogs do things for *dog* reasons, and everything they do works for them in some way or they wouldn't be doing it!

The Social Dog

Our pets descended from animals who lived in tightly knit, cooperative social groups. Though far removed in appearance and lifestyle from their ancestors, our dogs still relate in many of the same ways their wild relatives did. And in their relationships with one another, wild canids either lead or follow.

Canine ranking relationships are not about cruelty and power; they are about achievement and abilities. Competent dogs with high levels of drive and confidence step up, while deferring dogs step aside. But followers don't get the short end of the stick; they benefit from the security of having a more competent dog at the helm.

Our domestic dogs still measure themselves against other members of their group—us! Dog owners whose actions lead to positive results have willing, secure followers. But dogs may step up and fill the void or cut loose and do their own thing when their people fail to show capable leadership. When dogs are pushy, aggressive, and rude, or independent and unwilling, it's not because they have designs on the role of "master." It is more likely their owners failed to provide consistent leadership.

Dogs in training benefit from their handler's good leadership. Their education flows smoothly because they are impressed. Being in charge doesn't require you to physically dominate or punish your dog. You simply need to make some subtle changes in the way you relate to him every day.

Lead Your Pack!

Create schedules and structure daily activities. Dogs are creatures of habit and routines will create security. Feed meals at the same times each day and also try to schedule regular walks, training practices, and toilet outings. Your predictability will help your dog be patient.

Ask your dog to perform a task. Before releasing him to food or freedom, have him do something as simple as sit on command. Teach him that cooperation earns great results!

Give a release prompt (such as "let's go") when going through doors leading outside. This is a better idea than allowing your impatient pup to rush past you.

Pet your dog when he is calm, not when he is excited. Turn your touch into a tool that relaxes and settles.

Reward desirable rather than inappropriate behavior. Petting a jumping dog (who hasn't been invited up) reinforces jumping. Pet sitting dogs, and only invite lap dogs up after they've first "asked" by waiting for your invitation.

Replace personal punishment with positive reinforcement. Show a dog what *to do,* and motivate him to want to do it, and there will be no need to punish him for what he should *not do.* Dogs naturally follow, without the need for force or harshness.

Play creatively and appropriately. Your dog will learn the most about his social rank when he is playing with you. During play, dogs work to control toys and try to get the best of one another in a friendly way. The wrong sorts of play can create problems: For example, tug of war can lead to aggressiveness. Allowing your dog to control toys during play may result in possessive guarding when he has something he really values, such as a bone. Dogs who are chased during play may later run away from you when you approach to leash them. The right kinds of play will help increase your dog's social confidence while you gently assert your leadership.

How Dogs Learn (and How They Don't)

Dog training begins as a meeting of minds—yours and your dog's. Though the end goal may be to get your dog's body to behave in a specific way, training starts as a mind game. Your dog is learning all the time by observing the consequences of his actions and social interactions. He is always seeking out what he perceives as desirable and trying to avoid what he perceives as undesirable.

He will naturally repeat a behavior that either brings him more good stuff or makes bad stuff go away (these are both types of reinforcement). He will naturally avoid a behavior that brings him more bad stuff or makes the good stuff go away (these are both types of punishment).

Both reinforcement and punishment can be perceived as either the direct result of something the dog did himself, or as coming from an outside source.

Using Life's Rewards

Your best friend is smart and he is also cooperative. When the best things in life can only be had by working with you, your dog will view you as a facilitator. You unlock doors to all of the positively reinforcing experiences he values: his freedom, his friends at the park, food, affection, walks, and play. The trained dog accompanies you through those doors and waits to see what working with you will bring.

Rewarding your dog for good behavior is called positive reinforcement, and, as we've just seen, it increases the likelihood that he will repeat that behavior. The perfect reward is anything your dog wants that is safe and appropriate. Don't limit yourself to toys, treats, and things that come directly from you. Harness life's positives—barking at squirrels, chasing a falling leaf, bounding away from you at the dog park, pausing for a moment to sniff everything—and allow your dog to earn access to those things as rewards that come from cooperating with you. When he looks at you, when he sits, when he comes when you call—any prompted behavior can earn one of life's rewards. When he works with you, he earns the things he most appreciates; but when he tries to get those things on his own, he cannot. Rather than seeing you as someone who always says "no," your dog will view you as the one who says "let's go!" He will *want* to follow.

What About Punishment?

Not only is it unnecessary to personally punish dogs, it is abusive. No matter how convinced you are that your dog "knows right from wrong," in reality he will associate personal punishment with the punisher. The resulting cowering, "guilty"-looking postures are actually displays of submission and fear. Later,

Purely Positive Reinforcement

With positive training, we emphasize teaching dogs what they should do to earn reinforcements, rather than punishing them for unwanted behaviors.

- Focus on teaching "do" rather than "don't." For example, a sitting dog isn't jumping.
- Use positive reinforcers that are valuable to your dog and the situation: A tired dog values rest; a confined dog values freedom.
- Play (appropriately)!
- Be a consistent leader.
- Set your dog up for success by anticipating and preventing problems.
- Notice and reward desirable behavior, and give him lots of attention when he is being good.
- Train ethically. Use humane methods and equipment that do not frighten or hurt your dog.
- When you are angry, walk away and plan a positive strategy.
- Keep practice sessions short and sweet. Five to ten minutes, three to five times a day is best.

when the punisher isn't around and the coast is clear, the same behavior he was punished for—such as raiding a trash can—might bring a self-delivered, very tasty result. The punished dog hasn't learned not to misbehave; he has learned to not get caught.

Does punishment ever have a place in dog training? Many people will heartily insist it does not. But dog owners often get frustrated as they try to stick to the path of all-positive reinforcement. It sure sounds great, but is it realistic, or even natural, to *never* say "no" to your dog?

A wild dog's life is not *all* positive. Hunger and thirst are both examples of negative reinforcement; the resulting discomfort motivates the wild dog to seek food and water. He encounters natural aversives such as pesky insects; mats in his coat; cold days; rainy days; sweltering hot days; and occasional run-ins with thorns, brambles, skunks, bees, and other nastiness. These all affect his behavior, as he tries to avoid the bad stuff whenever possible. The wild dog also occasionally encounters social punishers from others in his group when he gets too pushy. Starting with a growl or a snap from Mom, and later some mild and ritualized discipline from other members of his four-legged family, he learns to modify behaviors that elicit grouchy responses.

Our pet dogs don't naturally experience all positive results either, because they learn from their surroundings and from social experiences with other dogs. Watch a group of pet dogs playing together and you'll see a very old educational system still being used. As they wrestle and attempt to assert themselves, you'll notice many mouth-on-neck moments. Their playful biting is inhibited, with no intention to cause harm, but their message is clear: "Say uncle or this could hurt more!"

Observing that punishment does occur in nature, some people may feel compelled to try to be like the big wolf with their pet dogs. Becoming aggressive or heavy-handed with your pet will backfire! Your dog will not be impressed, nor will he want to follow you. Punishment causes dogs to change their behavior to avoid or escape discomfort and threats. Threatened dogs will either become very passive and offer submissive, appeasing postures, attempt to flee, or rise to the occasion and fight back. When people personally punish their dogs in an angry manner, one of these three defensive mechanisms will be triggered. Which one depends on a dog's genetic temperament as well as his past social experiences. Since we don't want to make our pets feel the need to avoid or escape us, personal punishment has no place in our training.

Remote Consequences

Sometimes, however, all-positive reinforcement is just not enough. That's because not all reinforcement comes from us. An inappropriate behavior can be self-reinforcing—just doing it makes the dog feel better in some way, whether you are there to say "good boy!" or not. Some examples are eating garbage, pulling the stuffing out of your sofa, barking at passersby, or urinating on the floor.

Although you don't want to personally punish your dog, the occasional deterrent may be called for to help derail these kinds of self-rewarding misbehaviors. In these cases, mild forms of impersonal or remote punishment can be used as part of a correction. The goal isn't to make your dog feel bad or to "know he has done wrong," but to help redirect him to alternate behaviors that are more acceptable to you.

The Problems with Personal Punishment

- Personally punished dogs are not taught appropriate behaviors.
- Personally punished dogs only stop misbehaving when they are caught or interrupted, but they don't learn not to misbehave when they are alone.
- Personally punished dogs become shy, fearful, and distrusting.
- Personally punished dogs may become defensively aggressive.
- Personally punished dogs become suppressed and inhibited.
- Personally punished dogs become stressed, triggering stress-reducing behaviors that their owners interpret as acts of spite, triggering even more punishment.
- Personally punished dogs have stressed owners.
- Personally punished dogs may begin to repeat behaviors they have been taught will result in negative, but predictable, attention.
- Personally punished dogs are more likely to be given away than are positively trained dogs.

You do this by pairing a slightly startling, totally impersonal sound with an equally impersonal and *very mild* remote consequence. The impersonal sound might be a single shake of an empty plastic pop bottle with pennies in it, held out of your dog's sight. Or you could use a vocal expression such as "eh!" delivered with you looking *away* from your misbehaving dog.

Pair your chosen sound—the penny bottle or "eh!"—with either a slight tug on his collar or a sneaky spritz on the rump from a water bottle. Do this right *as* he touches something he should not; bad timing will confuse your dog and undermine your training success.

To keep things under your control and make sure you get the timing right, it's best to do this as a setup. "Accidentally" drop a shoe on the floor, and then help your dog learn some things are best avoided. As he sniffs the shoe say "eh!" without looking at him and give a *slight* tug against his collar. This sound will quickly become meaningful as a correction all by itself—sometimes after just one setup—making the tug correction obsolete. The tug lets your dog see that you were right; going for that shoe *was* a bad idea! Your wise dog will be more likely to heed your warning next time, and probably move closer to you where it's safe. Be a good friend and pick up the nasty shoe. He'll be relieved and you'll look heroic. Later, when he's home alone and encounters a stray shoe, he'll want to give it a wide berth.

Your negative marking sound will come in handy in the future, when your dog begins to venture down the wrong behavioral path. The goal is not to announce your disapproval or to threaten your dog. You are not telling him to stop or showing how *you* feel about his behavior. You are sounding a warning to a friend who's venturing off toward danger—"I wouldn't if I were you!" Suddenly, there is an abrupt, rather startling, noise! Now is the moment to redirect him and help him earn positive reinforcement. That interrupted behavior will become something he wants to avoid in the future, but he won't want to avoid you.

Practical Commands for Family Pets

Before you begin training your dog, let's look at some equipment you'll want to have on hand:

- **A buckle collar** is fine for most dogs. If your dog pulls *very* hard, try a head collar, a device similar to a horse halter that helps reduce pulling by turning the dog's head. *Do not* use a choke chain (sometimes called a training collar), because they cause physical harm even when used correctly.
- **Six-foot training leash and twenty-six–foot retractable leash.**
- **A few empty plastic soda bottles with about twenty pennies in each one.** This will be used to impersonally interrupt misbehaviors before redirecting dogs to more positive activities.
- **A favorite squeaky toy,** to motivate, attract attention, and reward your dog during training.

Baby Steps

Lure your dog to take just a few steps with you on the leash by being inviting and enthusiastic. Make sure you reward him for his efforts.

Allow your young pup to drag a short, lightweight leash attached to a buckle collar for a few *supervised* moments, several times each day. At first the leash may annoy him and he may jump around a bit trying to get away from it. Distract him with your squeaky toy or a bit of his kibble and he'll quickly get used to his new "tail."

Begin walking him on the leash by holding the end and following him. As he adapts, you can begin to assert gentle direct pressure to teach him to follow you. Don't jerk or yank, or he will become afraid to walk when the leash is on. If he becomes hesitant, squat down facing him and let him figure out that by moving toward you he is safe and secure. If he remains confused or frightened and doesn't come to you, go to him and help him understand that you provide safe harbor while he's on the leash. Then back away a few steps and try again to lure him to you. As he learns that you are the "home base," he'll want to follow when you walk a few steps, waiting for you to stop, squat down, and make him feel great.

So Attached to You!

The next step in training your dog—and this is a very important one—is to begin spending at least an hour or more each day with him on a four- to six-foot leash, held by or tethered to you. This training will increase his attachment to you—literally!—as you sit quietly or walk about, tending to your household business. When you are quiet, he'll learn it is time to settle; when you are active, he'll learn to move with you. Tethering also keeps him out of trouble when you are busy but still want his company. It is a great alternative to confining a dog, and can be used instead of crating any time you're home and need to slow him down a bit.

Rotating your dog from supervised freedom to tethered time to some quiet time in the crate or his gated area gives him a diverse and balanced day while he is learning. Two confined or tethered hours is the most you should require of your dog in one stretch, before changing to some supervised freedom, play, or a walk.

The dog in training may, at times, be stressed by all of the changes he is dealing with. Provide a stress outlet, such as a toy to chew on, when he is confined or tethered. He will settle into his quiet time more quickly and completely. Always be sure to provide several rounds of daily play and free time (in a fenced area or on your retractable leash) in addition to plenty of chewing materials.

Dog Talk

Dogs don't speak in words, but they do have a language—body language. They use postures, vocalizations, movements, facial gestures,

Tethering your dog is great way to keep him calm and under control, but still with you.

odors, and touch—usually with their mouths—to communicate what they are feeling and thinking.

We also "speak" using body language. We have quite an array of postures, movements, and facial gestures that accompany our touch and language as we attempt to communicate with our pets. And our dogs can quickly figure us out!

Alone, without associations, words are just noises. But, because we pair them with meaningful body language, our dogs make the connection. Dogs can really learn to understand much of what we *say*, if what we *do* at the same time is consistent.

The Positive Marker

Start your dog's education with one of the best tricks in dog training: Pair various positive reinforcers—food, a toy, touch—with a sound such as a click on a clicker (which you can get at the pet supply store) or a spoken word like "good!" or "yes!" This will enable you to later "mark" your dog's desirable behaviors.

It seems too easy: Just say "yes!" and give the dog his toy. (Or use whatever sound and reward you have chosen.) Later, when you make your marking sound right at the instant your dog does the right thing, he will know you are going to be giving him something good for that particular action. And he'll be eager to repeat the behavior to hear you mark it again!

Next, you must teach your dog to understand the meaning of cues you'll be using to ask him to perform specific behaviors. This is easy, too. Does he already do things you might like him to do on command? Of course! He lies down, he sits, he picks things up, he drops them again, he comes to you. All of the behaviors you'd like to control are already part of your dog's natural repertoire. The trick is getting him to offer those behaviors when you ask for them. And that means you have to teach him to associate a particular behavior on his part with a particular behavior on your part.

Sit Happens

Teach your dog an important new rule: From now on, he is only touched and petted when he is either sitting or lying down. You won't need to ask him to sit; in fact, you should not. Just keeping him tethered near you so there isn't much to do but stand, be ignored, or settle, and wait until sit happens.

He may pester you a bit, but be stoic and unresponsive. Starting now, when *you* are sitting down, a sitting dog is the only one you see and pay attention to. He will eventually sit, and as he does, attach the word "sit"—but don't be too excited or he'll jump right back up. Now mark with your positive sound that promises something good, then reward him with a slow, quiet, settling pet.

Training requires consistent reinforcement. Ask others to also wait until your dog is sitting and calm to touch him, and he will associate being petted with being relaxed. Be sure you train your dog to associate everyone's touch with quiet bonding.

Reinforcing "Sit" as a Command

Since your dog now understands one concept of working for a living—sit to earn petting—you can begin to shape and reinforce his desire to sit. Hold toys, treats, his bowl of food, and turn into a statue. But don't prompt him to sit! Instead, remain frozen and unavailable, looking somewhere out into space, over his head. He will put on a bit of a show, trying to get a response from you, and may offer various behaviors, but only one will push your button—sitting. Wait for him to offer the "right" behavior, and when he does, you unfreeze. Say "sit," then mark with an excited "good!" and give him the toy or treat with a release command—"OK!"

When you notice spontaneous sits occurring, be sure to take advantage of those free opportunities to make your command sequence meaningful and positive. Say "sit" as you observe sit happen—then mark with "good!" and praise, pet, or reward the dog. Soon, every time you look at your dog he'll be sitting and looking right back at you!

Now, after thirty days of purely positive practice, it's time to give him a test. When he is just walking around doing his own thing, suddenly ask him to sit. He'll probably do it right away. If he doesn't, do *not* repeat your command, or you'll just undermine its meaning ("sit" means sit *now;* the command is not "sit, sit, sit, sit"). Instead, get something he likes and let him know you have it. Wait for him to offer the sit—he will—then say "sit!" and complete your marking and rewarding sequence.

OK

"OK" will probably rate as one of your dog's favorite words. It's like the word "recess" to schoolchildren. It is the word used to release your dog from a command. You can introduce "OK" during your "sit" practice. When he gets up from a sit, say "OK" to tell him the sitting is finished. Soon that sound will mean "freedom."

Make it even more meaningful and positive. Whenever he spontaneously bounds away, say "OK!" Squeak a toy, and when he notices and shows interest, toss it for him.

Down

I've mentioned that you should only pet your dog when he is either sitting or lying down. Now, using the approach I've just introduced for "sit," teach your dog to lie down. You will be a statue, and hold something he would like to get but that you'll only release to a dog who is lying down. It helps to lower the desired item to the floor in front of him, still not speaking and not letting him have it until he offers you the new behavior you are seeking.

Lower your dog's reward to the floor to help him figure out what behavior will earn him his reward.

He may offer a sit and then wait expectantly, but you must make him keep searching for the new trick that triggers your generosity. Allow your dog to experiment and find the right answer, even if he has to search around for it first. When he lands on "down" and learns it is another behavior that works, he'll offer it more quickly the next time.

Don't say "down" until he lies down, to tightly associate your prompt with the correct behavior. To say "down, down, down" as he is sitting, looking at you, or pawing at the toy would make "down" mean those behaviors instead! Whichever behavior he offers, a training opportunity has been created. Once you've attached and shaped both sitting and lying down, you can ask for both behaviors with your verbal prompts, "sit" or "down." Be sure to only reinforce the "correct" reply!

Stay

"Stay" can easily be taught as an extension of what you've already been practicing. To teach "stay," you follow the entire sequence for reinforcing a "sit" or "down," except you wait a bit longer before you give the release word, "OK!" Wait a second or two longer during each practice before saying "OK!" and releasing your dog to the positive reinforcer (toy, treat, or one of life's other rewards).

You can step on the leash to help your dog understand the down-stay, but only do this when he is already lying down. You don't want to hurt him!

If he gets up before you've said "OK," you have two choices: pretend the release was your idea and quickly interject "OK!" as he breaks; or, if he is more experienced and practiced, mark the behavior with your correction sound— "eh!"— and then gently put him back on the spot, wait for him to lie down, and begin again. Be sure the next three practices are a success. Ask him to wait for just a second, and release him before he can be wrong. You need to keep your dog feeling like more of a success than a failure as you begin to test his training in increasingly more distracting and difficult situations.

As he gets the hang of it—he stays until you say "OK"—you can gradually push for longer times—up to a minute on a sit-stay, and up to three minutes on a down-stay. You can also gradually add distractions and work in new environments. To add a minor self-correction for the down-stay, stand on the dog's leash after he lies down, allowing about three inches of slack. If he tries to get up before you've said "OK," he'll discover it doesn't work.

Do not step on the leash to make your dog lie down! This could badly hurt his neck, and will destroy his trust in you. Remember, we are teaching our dogs to make the best choices, not inflicting our answers upon them!

Come

Rather than thinking of "come" as an action—"come to me"—think of it as a place—"the dog is sitting in front of me, facing me." Since your dog by now really likes sitting to earn your touch and other positive reinforcement, he's likely to sometimes sit directly in front of you, facing you, all on his own. When this happens, give it a specific name: "come."

Now follow the rest of the training steps you have learned to make him like doing it and reinforce the behavior by practicing it any chance you get. Anything your dog wants and likes could be earned as a result of his first offering the sit-in-front known as "come."

You can help guide him into the right location. Use your hands as "landing gear" and pat the insides of your legs at his nose level. Do this while backing up a bit, to help him maneuver to the straight-in-front, facing-you position. Don't say the

Pat the insides of your legs to show your dog exactly where you like him to sit when you say "come."

word "come" while he's maneuvering, because he hasn't! You are trying to make "come" the end result, not the work in progress.

You can also help your dog by marking his movement in the right direction: Use your positive sound or word to promise he is getting warm. When he finally sits facing you, enthusiastically say "come," mark again with your positive word, and release him with an enthusiastic "OK!" Make it so worth his while, with lots of play and praise, that he can't wait for you to ask him to come again!

Building a Better Recall

Practice, practice, practice. Now, practice some more. Teach your dog that all good things in life hinge upon him first sitting in front of you in a behavior named "come." When you think he really has got it, test him by asking him to "come" as you gradually add distractions and change locations. Expect setbacks as you make these changes and practice accordingly. Lower your expectations and make his task easier so he is able to get it right. Use those distractions as rewards, when they are appropriate. For example, let him check out the interesting leaf that blew by as a reward for first coming to you and ignoring it.

Add distance and call your dog to come while he is on his retractable leash. If he refuses and sits looking at you blankly, *do not* jerk, tug, "pop," or reel him in. Do nothing! It is his move; wait to see what behavior he offers. He'll either begin to approach (mark the behavior with an excited "good!"), sit and do nothing (just keep waiting), or he'll try to move in some direction other than toward you. If he tries to leave, use your correction marker—"eh!"—and bring him to a stop by letting him walk to the end of the leash, *not* by jerking him. Now walk to him in a neutral manner, and don't jerk or show any disapproval. Gently bring him back to the spot where he was when you called him, then back away and face him, still waiting and not reissuing your command. Let him keep examining his options until he finds the one that works—yours!

If you have practiced everything I've suggested so far and given your dog a chance to really learn what "come" means, he is well aware of what you want and is quite intelligently weighing all his options. The only way he'll know your way is the one that works is to be allowed to examine his other choices and discover that they *don't* work.

Sooner or later every dog tests his training. Don't be offended or angry when your dog tests you. No matter how positive you've made it, he won't always want to do everything you ask, every time. When he explores the "what happens if I don't" scenario, your training is being strengthened. He will discover through his own process of trial and error that the best—and only—way out of a command he really doesn't feel compelled to obey is to obey it.

Let's Go

Many pet owners wonder if they can retain control while walking their dogs and still allow at least some running in front, sniffing, and playing. You might worry that allowing your dog occasional freedom could result in him expecting it all the time, leading to a testy, leash-straining walk. It's possible for both parties on the leash to have an enjoyable experience by implementing and reinforcing well-thought-out training techniques.

Give your dog slack on his leash as you walk and let him make the decision to walk with you.

Begin by making word associations you'll use on your walks. Give the dog some slack on the leash, and as he starts to walk away from you say "OK" and begin to follow him.

Do not let him drag you; set the pace even when he is being given a turn at being the leader. Whenever he starts to pull, just come to a standstill and refuse to move (or refuse to allow him to continue forward) until there is slack in the leash. Do this correction without saying anything at all. When he isn't pulling, you may decide to just stand still and let him sniff about within the range the slack leash allows, or you may even mosey along following him. After a few minutes of "recess," it is time to work. Say something like "that's it" or "time's up," close the distance between you and your dog, and touch him.

When your dog catches up with you, make sure you let him know what a great dog he is!

Next say "let's go" (or whatever command you want to use to mean "follow me as we walk"). Turn and walk off, and, if he follows, mark his behavior with "good!" Then stop,

Intersperse periods of attentive walking, where your dog is on a shorter leash, with periods on a slack leash, where he is allowed to look and sniff around.

squat down, and let him catch you. Make him glad he did! Start again, and do a few transitions as he gets the hang of your follow-the-leader game, speeding up, slowing down, and trying to make it fun. When you stop, he gets to catch up and receive some deserved positive reinforcement. Don't forget that's the reason he is following you, so be sure to make it worth his while!

Require him to remain attentive to you. Do not allow sniffing, playing, eliminating, or pulling during your time as leader on a walk. If he seems to get distracted—which, by the way, is the main reason dogs walk poorly with their people— change direction or pace without saying a word. Just help him realize "oops, I lost track of my human." Do not jerk his neck and say "heel"—this will make the word "heel" mean pain in the neck and will not encourage him to cooperate with you. Don't repeat "let's go," either. He needs to figure out that it is his job to keep track of and follow you if he wants to earn the positive benefits you provide.

The best reward you can give a dog for performing an attentive, controlled walk is a few minutes of walking without all of the controls. Of course, he must remain on a leash even during the "recess" parts of the walk, but allowing him to discriminate between attentive following—"let's go"—and having a few moments of relaxation—"OK"—will increase his willingness to work.

Training for Attention

Your dog pretty much has a one-track mind. Once he is focused on something, everything else is excluded. This can be great, for instance, when he's focusing on you! But it can also be dangerous if, for example, his attention is riveted on the bunny he is chasing and he does not hear you call—that is, not unless he has been trained to pay attention when you say his name.

When you say your dog's name, you'll want him to make eye contact with you. Begin teaching this by making yourself so intriguing that he can't help but look.

When you call your dog's name, you will again be seeking a specific response—eye contact. The best way to teach this is to trigger his alerting response by making a noise with your mouth, such as whistling or a kissing sound, and then immediately doing something he'll find very intriguing.

You can play a treasure hunt game to help teach him to regard his name as a request for attention. As a bonus, you can reinforce the rest of his new vocabulary at the same time.

Treasure Hunt

Make a kissing sound, then jump up and find a dog toy or dramatically raid the fridge and rather noisily eat a piece of cheese. After doing this twice, make a kissing sound and then look at your dog.

Of course he is looking at you! He is waiting to see if that sound—the kissing sound—means you're going to go hunting again. After all, you're so good at it! Because he is looking, say his name, mark with "good," then go hunting and find his toy. Release it to him with an "OK." At any point if he follows you, attach your "let's go!" command; if he leaves you, give permission with "OK."

Using this approach, he cannot be wrong—any behavior your dog offers can be named. You can add things like "take it" when he picks up a toy, and "thank you" when he happens to drop one. Many opportunities to make your new vocabulary meaningful and positive can be found within this simple training game.

Problems to watch out for when teaching the treasure hunt:

- You really do not want your dog to come to you when you call his name (later, when you try to engage his attention to ask him to stay, he'll already be on his way toward you). You just want him to look at you.
- Saying "watch me, watch me" doesn't teach your dog to *offer* his attention. It just makes you a background noise.
- Don't lure your dog's attention with the reward. Get his attention and then reward him for looking. Try holding a toy in one hand with your arm stretched out to your side. Wait until he looks at you rather than the toy. Now say his name then mark with "good!" and release the toy. As he goes for it, say "OK."

To get your dog's attention, try holding his toy with your arm out to your side. Wait until he looks at you, then mark the moment and give him the toy.

Teaching Cooperation

Never punish your dog for failing to obey you or try to punish him into compliance. Bribing, repeating yourself, and doing a behavior for him all avoid the real issue of dog training—his will. He must be helped to be willing, not made to achieve tasks. Good dog training helps your dog want to obey. He learns that he can gain what he values most through cooperation and compliance, and can't gain those things any other way.

Your dog is learning to *earn,* rather than expect, the good things in life. And you've become much more important to him than you were before. Because you are allowing him to experiment and learn, he doesn't have to be forced, manipulated, or bribed. When he wants something, he can gain it by cooperating with you. One of those "somethings"—and a great reward you shouldn't underestimate—is your positive attention, paid to him with love and sincere approval!

Chapter 10

Housetraining Your Miniature Schnauzer

Excerpted from Housetraining: An Owner's Guide to a Happy Healthy Pet, 1st edition, *by September Morn*

By the time puppies are about 3 weeks old, they start to follow their mother around. When they are a few steps away from their clean sleeping area, the mama dog stops. The pups try to nurse but Mom won't allow it. The pups mill around in frustration, then nature calls and they all urinate and defecate here, away from their bed. The mother dog returns to the nest, with her brood waddling behind her. Their first housetraining lesson has been a success.

The next one to housetrain puppies should be their breeder. The breeder watches as the puppies eliminate, then deftly removes the soiled papers and replaces them with clean papers before the pups can traipse back through their messes. He has wisely arranged the puppies' space so their bed, food, and drinking water are as far away from the elimination area as possible. This way, when the pups follow their mama, they will move away from their sleeping and eating area before eliminating. This habit will help the pups be easily housetrained.

Your Housetraining Shopping List

While your puppy's mother and breeder are getting her started on good housetraining habits, you'll need to do some shopping. If you have all the essentials in place before your dog arrives, it will be easier to help her learn the rules from day one.

Newspaper: The younger your puppy and larger her breed, the more newspapers you'll need. Newspaper is absorbent, abundant, cheap, and convenient.

Puddle Pads: If you prefer not to stockpile newspaper, a commercial alternative is puddle pads. These thick paper pads can be purchased under several trade names at pet supply stores. The pads have waterproof backing, so puppy urine doesn't seep through onto the floor. Their disadvantages are that they will cost you more than newspapers and that they contain plastics that are not biodegradable.

Poop Removal Tool: There are several types of poop removal tools available. Some are designed with a separate pan and rake, and others have the handles hinged like scissors. Some scoops need two hands for operation, while others are designed for one-handed use. Try out the different brands at your pet supply store. Put a handful of pebbles or dog kibble on the floor and then pick them up with each type of scoop to determine which works best for you.

Good breeders get their pups started off right, in housetraining as in all aspects of their early care.

Plastic Bags: When you take your dog outside your yard, you *must* pick up after her. Dog waste is unsightly, smelly, and can harbor disease. In many cities and towns, the law mandates dog owners clean up pet waste deposited on public ground. Picking up after your dog using a plastic bag scoop is simple. Just put your hand inside the bag, like a mitten, and then grab the droppings. Turn the bag inside out, tie the top, and that's that.

Crate: To housetrain a puppy, you will need some way to confine her when you're unable to supervise. A dog crate is a secure way to confine your dog for short periods during the day and to use as a comfortable bed at night. Crates come in wire mesh and in plastic. The wire ones are foldable to store flat in a smaller space. The plastic ones are more cozy, draft-free, and quiet, and are approved for airline travel.

Baby Gates: Since you shouldn't crate a dog for more than an hour or two at a time during the day, baby gates are a good way to limit your dog's freedom in the house. Be sure the baby gates you use are safe. The old-fashioned wooden, expanding lattice type has seriously injured a number of children by collapsing and trapping a leg, arm, or neck. That type of gate can hurt a puppy, too, so use the modern grid type gates instead. You'll need more than one baby gate if you have several doorways to close off.

Exercise Pen: Portable exercise pens are great when you have a young pup or a small dog. These metal or plastic pens are made of rectangular panels that are hinged together. The pens are freestanding, sturdy, foldable, and can be carried like a suitcase. You could set one up in your kitchen as the pup's daytime corral, and then take it outdoors to contain your pup while you garden or just sit and enjoy the day.

Enzymatic Cleaner: All dogs make housetraining mistakes. Accept this and be ready for it by buying an enzymatic cleaner made especially for pet accidents. Dogs like to eliminate where they have done it before, and lingering smells lead them to those spots. Ordinary household cleaners may remove all the odors you can smell, but only an enzymatic cleaner will remove everything your dog can smell.

The First Day

Housetraining is a matter of establishing good habits in your dog. That means you never want her to learn anything she will eventually have to unlearn. Start off housetraining on the right foot by teaching your dog that you prefer her to

Don't Overuse the Crate

A crate serves well as a dog's overnight bed, but you should not leave the dog in her crate for more than an hour or two during the day. Throughout the day, she needs to play and exercise. She is likely to want to drink some water and will undoubtedly eliminate. Confining your dog all day will give her no option but to soil her crate. This is not just unpleasant for you and the dog, but it reinforces bad cleanliness habits. And crating a pup for the whole day is abusive. Don't do it.

eliminate outside. Designate a potty area in your backyard (if you have one) or in the street in front of your home and take your dog to it as soon as you arrive home. Let her sniff a bit and, when she squats to go, give the action a name: "potty" or "do it" or anything else you won't be embarrassed to say in public. Eventually your dog will associate that word with the act and will eliminate on command. When she's finished, praise her with "good potty!"

That first day, take your puppy out to the potty area frequently. Although she may not eliminate every time, you are establishing a routine: You take her to her spot, ask her to eliminate, and praise her when she does.

Just before bedtime, take your dog to her potty area once more. Stand by and wait until she produces. Do not put your dog to bed for the night until she has eliminated. Be patient and calm. This is not the time to play with or excite your dog. If she's too excited, a pup not only won't eliminate, she probably won't want to sleep either.

Most dogs, even young ones, will not soil their beds if they can avoid it. For this reason, a sleeping crate can be a tremendous help during housetraining. Being crated at night can help a dog develop the muscles that control elimination. So after your dog has emptied out, put her to bed in her crate.

A good place to put your dog's sleeping crate is near your own bed. Dogs are pack animals, so they feel safer sleeping with others in a common area. In your bedroom, the pup will be near you and you'll be close enough to hear when she wakes during the night and needs to eliminate.

Pups under 4 months old often are not able to hold their urine all night. If your puppy has settled down to sleep but awakens and fusses a few hours later, she probably needs to go out. For the best housetraining progress, take your pup to her elimination area whenever she needs to go, even in the wee hours of the morning.

Make sure your yard is safe and secure for potty breaks. Miniature Schnauzers are small dogs and can squeeze into tight spots.

Your pup may soil in her crate if you ignore her late night urgency. It's unfair to let this happen, and it sends the wrong message about your expectations for cleanliness. Resign yourself to this midnight outing and just get up and take the pup out. Your pup will outgrow this need soon and will learn in the process that she can count on you, and you'll wake happily each morning to a clean dog.

The next morning, the very first order of business is to take your pup out to eliminate. Don't forget to take her to her special potty spot, ask her to eliminate, and then praise her when she does. After your pup empties out in the morning, give her breakfast, and then take her to her potty area again. After that, she shouldn't need to eliminate again right away, so you can allow her some free playtime. Keep an eye on the pup though, because when she pauses in play she may need to go potty. Take her to the right spot, give the command, and praise if she produces.

Confine Your Pup

A pup or dog who has not finished housetraining should *never* be allowed the run of the house unattended. A new dog (especially a puppy) with unlimited access to your house will make her own choices about where to eliminate.

Vigilance during your new dog's first few weeks in your home will pay big dividends. Every potty mistake delays housetraining progress; every success speeds it along.

Prevent problems by setting up a controlled environment for your new pet. A good place for a puppy corral is often the kitchen. Kitchens almost always have waterproof or easily cleaned floors, which is a distinct asset with leaky pups. A bathroom, laundry room, or enclosed porch could be used for a puppy corral, but the kitchen is generally the best location. Kitchens are a meeting place and a hub of activity for many families, and a puppy will learn better manners when she is socialized thoroughly with family, friends, and nice strangers.

The way you structure your pup's corral area is very important. Her bed, food, and water should be at the opposite end of the corral from the potty area. When you first get your pup, spread newspaper over the rest of the floor of her playpen corral. Lay the papers at least four pages thick and be sure to overlap the edges. As you note the pup's progress, you can remove the papers nearest the sleeping and eating corner. Gradually decrease the size of the papered area until only the end where you want the pup to eliminate is covered. If you will be training your dog to eliminate outside, place newspaper at the end of the corral that is closest to the door that leads outdoors. That way as she moves away from the clean area to the papered area, the pup will also form the habit of heading toward the door to go out.

Maintain a scent marker for the pup's potty area by reserving a small soiled piece of paper when you clean up. Place this piece, with her scent of urine, under the top sheet of the clean papers you spread. This will cue your pup where to eliminate.

Most dog owners use a combination of indoor papers and outdoor elimination areas. When the pup is left by herself in the corral, she can potty on the ever-present newspaper. When you are available to take the pup outside, she can do her business in the outdoor spot. It is not difficult to switch a pup from indoor paper training to outdoor elimination. Owners of large pups often switch early, but potty papers are still useful

> ### TIP
>
> **Water**
>
> Make sure your dog has access to clean water at all times. Limiting the amount of water a dog drinks is not necessary for housetraining success and can be very dangerous. A dog needs water to digest food, to maintain a proper body temperature and proper blood volume, and to clean her system of toxins and wastes. A healthy dog will automatically drink the right amount. Do not restrict water intake. Controlling your dog's access to water is not the key to housetraining her; controlling her access to everything else in your home is.

You can teach your dog to eliminate in your yard or outside in the street. No matter what spot you pick, be sure to pick up after her.

if the pup spends time in her indoor corral while you're away. Use the papers as long as your pup needs them. If you come home and they haven't been soiled, you are ahead.

When setting up your pup's outdoor yard, put the lounging area as far away as possible from the potty area, just as with the indoor corral setup. People with large yards, for example, might leave a patch unmowed at the edge of the lawn to serve as the dog's elimination area. Other dog owners teach the dog to relieve herself in a designated corner of a deck or patio. For an apartment-dwelling city dog, the outdoor potty area might be a tiny balcony or the curb. Each dog owner has somewhat different expectations for their dog. Teach your dog to eliminate in a spot that suits your environment and lifestyle.

Be sure to pick up droppings in your yard at least once a day. Dogs have a natural desire to stay far away from their own excrement, and if too many piles litter the ground, your dog won't want to walk through it and will start eliminating elsewhere. Leave just one small piece of feces in the potty area to remind your dog where the right spot is located.

To help a pup adapt to the change from indoors to outdoors, take one of her potty papers outside to the new elimination area. Let the pup stand on the paper when she goes potty outdoors. Each day for four days, reduce the size of the paper by half. By the fifth day, the pup, having used a smaller and smaller piece of paper to stand on, will probably just go to that spot and eliminate.

Take your pup to her outdoor potty place frequently throughout the day. A puppy can hold her urine for only about as many hours as her age in months, and will move her bowels as many times a day as she eats. So a 2-month-old pup will urinate about every two hours, while at 4 months she can manage about four hours between piddles. Pups vary somewhat in their rate of development, so this is not a hard and fast rule. It does, however, present a realistic idea of how long a pup can be left without access to a potty place. Past 4 months, her potty trips will be less frequent.

When you take the dog outdoors to her spot, keep her leashed so that she won't wander away. Stand quietly and let her sniff around in the designated area. If your pup starts to leave before she has eliminated, gently lead her back and remind her to go. If your pup sniffs at the spot, praise her calmly, say the command word, and just wait. If she produces, praise serenely, then give her time to sniff around a little more. She may not be finished, so give her time to go again before allowing her to play and explore her new home.

If you find yourself waiting more than five minutes for your dog to potty, take her back inside. Watch your pup carefully for twenty minutes, not giving her any opportunity to slip away to eliminate unnoticed. If you are too busy to watch the pup, put her in her crate. After twenty minutes, take her to the outdoor potty spot again and tell her what to do. If you're unsuccessful after five minutes, crate the dog again. Give her another chance to eliminate in fifteen or twenty minutes. Eventually, she will have to go.

Watch Your Pup

Be vigilant and don't let the pup make a mistake in the house. Each time you successfully anticipate elimination and take your pup to the potty spot, you'll move a step closer to your goal. Stay aware of your puppy's needs. If you ignore the pup, she will make mistakes and you'll be cleaning up more messes.

Keep a chart of your new dog's elimination behavior for the first three or four days. Jot down what times she eats, sleeps, and eliminates. After several days a pattern will emerge that can help you determine your pup's body rhythms. Most dogs tend to eliminate at fairly regular intervals. Once you know your new dog's natural rhythms, you'll be able to anticipate her needs and schedule appropriate potty outings.

Understanding the meanings of your dog's postures can also help you win the battle of the puddle. When your dog is getting ready to eliminate, she will

Pups often need to go potty after a nap.

display a specific set of postures. The sooner you can learn to read these signals, the cleaner your floor will stay.

A young puppy who feels the urge to eliminate may start to sniff the ground and walk in a circle. If the pup is very young, she may simply squat and go. All young puppies, male or female, squat to urinate. If you are housetraining a pup under 4 months of age, regardless of sex, watch for the beginnings of a squat as the signal to rush the pup to the potty area.

When a puppy is getting ready to defecate, she may run urgently back and forth or turn in a circle while sniffing or starting to squat. If defecation is imminent, the pup's anus may protrude or open slightly. When she starts to go, the pup will squat and hunch her back, her tail sticking straight out behind. There is no mistaking this posture; nothing else looks like this. If your pup takes this position, take her to her potty area. Hurry! You may have to carry her to get there in time.

A young puppy won't have much time between feeling the urge and actually eliminating, so you'll have to be quick to note her postural clues and intercept your pup in time. Pups from 3 to 6 months have a few seconds more between the urge and the act than younger ones do. The older your pup, the more time you'll have to get her to the potty area after she begins the posture signals that alert you to her need.

Accidents Happen

If you see your pup about to eliminate somewhere other than the designated area, interrupt her immediately. Say "wait, wait, wait!" or clap your hands loudly to startle her into stopping. Carry the pup, if she's still small enough, or take her collar and lead her to the correct area. Once your dog is in the potty area, give her the command to eliminate. Use a friendly voice for the command, then wait patiently for her to produce. The pup may be tense because you've just startled her and may have to relax a bit before she's able to eliminate. When she does her job, include the command word in the praise you give ("good potty").

The old-fashioned way of housetraining involved punishing a dog's mistakes even before she knew what she was supposed to do. Puppies were punished for breaking rules they didn't understand about functions they couldn't control.

This was not fair. While your dog is new to housetraining, there is no need or excuse for punishing her mistakes. Your job is to take the dog to the potty area just before she needs to go, especially with pups under 3 months old. If you aren't watching your pup closely enough and she has an accident, don't punish the puppy for your failure to anticipate her needs. It's not the pup's fault; it's yours.

In any case, punishment is not an effective tool for housetraining most dogs. Many will react to punishment by hiding puddles and feces where you won't find them right away (like behind the couch or under the desk). This eventually may lead to punishment after the fact, which leads to more hiding, and so on.

Instead of punishing for mistakes, stay a step ahead of potty accidents by learning to anticipate your pup's needs. Accompany your dog to the designated potty area when she needs to go. Tell her what you want her to do and praise her when she goes. This will work wonders. Punishment won't be necessary if you are a good teacher.

What happens if you come upon a mess after the fact? Some trainers say a dog can't remember having eliminated, even a few moments after she has done so. This is not true. The fact is that urine and feces carry a dog's unique scent, which she (and every other dog) can instantly recognize. So, if you happen upon a potty mistake after the fact you can still use it to teach your dog.

But remember, no punishment! Spanking, hitting, shaking, or scaring a puppy for having a housetraining accident is confusing and counter-productive. Spend your energy instead on positive forms of teaching.

Take your pup and a paper towel to the mess. Point to the urine or feces and calmly tell your puppy, "no potty here." Then scoop or sop up the accident with the paper towel. Take the evidence and the pup to the approved potty area. Drop the mess on the ground and tell the dog, "good potty here," as if she had done the deed in the right place. If your pup sniffs at the evidence, praise her calmly. If the accident happened very recently your dog may not have to go yet, but

Stay ahead of accidents by anticipating your dog's needs and taking her out for frequent potty breaks.

wait with her a few minutes anyway. If she eliminates, praise her. Afterwards, go finish cleaning up the mess.

Soon the puppy will understand that there is a place where you are pleased about elimination and other places where you are not. Praising for elimination in the approved place will help your pup remember the rules.

Scheduling Basics

With a new puppy in the home, don't be surprised if your rising time is suddenly a little earlier than you've been accustomed to. Puppies have earned a reputation as very early risers. When your pup wakes you at the crack of dawn, you will have to get up and take her to her elimination spot. Be patient. When your dog is an adult, she may enjoy sleeping in as much as you do.

At the end of the chapter, you'll find a typical housetraining schedule for puppies aged 10 weeks to 6 months. (To find schedules for younger and older pups, and for adult dogs, visit this book's companion web site.) It's fine to adjust the rising times when using this schedule, but you should not adjust the intervals between feedings and potty outings unless your pup's behavior justifies a change. Your puppy can only meet your expectations in housetraining if you help her learn the rules.

What goes in must come out. Schedule your dog's meals so you can schedule the potty breaks.

The schedule for puppies is devised with the assumption that someone will be home most of the time with the pup. That would be the best scenario, of course, but is not always possible. You may be able to ease the problems of a latchkey pup by having a neighbor or friend look in on the pup at noon and take her to eliminate. A better solution might be hiring a pet sitter to drop by midday. A professional pet sitter will be knowledgeable about companion animals and can give your pup high-quality care and socialization. Some can even help train your pup in both potty manners and basic obedience. Ask your veterinarian and your dog-owning friends to recommend a good pet sitter.

If you must leave your pup alone during her early housetraining period, be sure to cover the entire floor of her corral with thick layers of overlapping newspaper. If you come home to messes in the puppy corral, just clean them up. Be patient—she's still a baby.

Use this schedule (and the ones on the companion web site) as a basic plan to help prevent housetraining accidents. Meanwhile, use your own powers of observation to discover how to best modify the basic schedule to fit your dog's unique needs. Each dog is an individual and will have her own rhythms, and each dog is reliable at a different age.

Schedule for Pups 10 Weeks to 6 Months

7:00 a.m.	Get up and take the puppy from her sleeping crate to her potty spot.
7:15	Clean up last night's messes, if any.
7:30	Food and fresh water.
7:45	Pick up the food bowl. Take the pup to her potty spot; wait and praise.
8:00	The pup plays around your feet while you have your breakfast.
9:00	Potty break (younger pups may not be able to wait this long).
9:15	Play and obedience practice.
10:00	Potty break.
10:15	The puppy is in her corral with safe toys to chew and play with.
11:30	Potty break (younger pups may not be able to wait this long).
11:45	Food and fresh water.

continues

Schedule for Pups 10 Weeks to 6 Months (continued)

12:00 p.m.	Pick up the food bowl and take the pup to her potty spot.
12:15	The puppy is in her corral with safe toys to chew and play with.
1:00	Potty break (younger pups may not be able to wait this long).
1:15	Put the pup on a leash and take her around the house with you.
3:30	Potty break (younger pups may not be able to wait this long).
3:45	Put the pup in her corral with safe toys and chews for solitary play and/or a nap.
4:45	Potty break.
5:00	Food and fresh water.
5:15	Potty break.
5:30	The pup may play nearby (either leashed or in her corral) while you prepare your evening meal.
7:00	Potty break.
7:15	Leashed or closely watched, the pup may play and socialize with family and visitors.
9:15	Potty break (younger pups may not be able to wait this long).
10:45	Last chance to potty.
11:00	Put the pup to bed in her crate for the night.

Appendix

Learning More About Your Miniature Schnauzer

Some Good Books

About Miniature Schnauzers

Gallant, Johan, *The World of Schnauzers,* Alpine Publications, 1996.
Kiedrowski, Dan, *The New Miniature Schnauzer,* Howell Book House, 1997.
Newman, Peter, *Miniature Schnauzer Today,* Howell Book House, 1998.

Care and Health

Arden, Darlene, *The Angell Memorial Animal Hospital Book of Wellness and Preventive Care for Dogs,* McGraw-Hill, 2002.
Bamberger, Michelle, DVM, *Help! The Quick Guide to First Aid for Your Dog,* Howell Book House, 1995.
Messonnier, Shawn, DVM, *Natural Health Bible for Dogs and Cats: Your A–Z Guide to Over 200 Conditions, Herbs, Vitamins, and Supplements,* Three Rivers Press, 2001.

About Training

Benjamin, Carol Lea, *Mother Knows Best,* Howell Book House, 1985.
Evans, Job Michael, *People, Pooches and Problems,* Howell Book House, 2001.
McConnell, Patricia, *The Other End of the Leash,* Ballantine Books, 2003.
Smith, Cheryl S., *The Rosetta Bone,* Howell Book House, 2004.

Canine Activities

Davis, Kathy Diamond, *Therapy Dogs,* Howell Book House, 1992.

Hall, Lynn, *Dog Showing for Beginners,* Howell Book House, 1994.

LaBelle, Charlene G., *Backpacking with Your Dog,* Alpine Publications, 1993.

Simmons-Moake, Jane, *Agility Training: The Fun Sport for All Dogs,* Howell Book House, 1991.

Volhard, Jack and Wendy, *The Canine Good Citizen: Every Dog Can Be One,* Howell Book House, 1997.

Magazines

AKC Gazette and
AKC Family Dog
American Kennel Club
260 Madison Avenue
New York, NY 10016
(212) 696-8200
www.akc.org

The Bark
2810 8th Street
Berkeley, CA 94710
(510) 704-0827
www.thebark.com

Dog Fancy
P.O. Box 37185
Boone, IA 50037-0185
(800) 896-4939
www.dogfancy.com

DogWorld
P.O. Box 37186
Boone, IA 50037-0186
(800) 896-4939
www.dogworldmag.com

Just Terriers
Just Us Dog Publications
P.O. Box 518
Trappe, MD 21673
(708) 878-2539
www.justterriers.com

Publications

Miniature Schnauzer Grooming Chart
Illustrated Discussion of the Miniature Schnauzer Standard
The History of the American Miniature Schnauzer Club
AMSC Publication and Literature
P.O. Box 17493
West Palm Beach, FL 33416
www.amsc.us

Clubs and Registries

There are numerous all-breed, individual breed, canine sporting, and other special-interest dog clubs across the country. The American Kennel Club can provide you with a list of clubs in your area.

The American Kennel Club (AKC)
260 Madison Avenue
New York, NY 10016
(212) 696-8200
www.akc.org

American Miniature Schnauzer Club
Ms. Terrie Houck
105 Fite's Creek Road
Mount Holly, NC 28120-1149
(704) 827-6544
www.amsc.us
e-mail: secretary@amsc.us

Web Sites

Miniature Schnauzer Club of Canada
www.mscc.ca
Official national breed club for Miniature Schnauzer enthusiasts in Canada, promoting the benefit and protection of the breed through responsible ownership.

Miniature Schnauzer Rescue of Houston
www.miniatureschnauzerrescue.org
The site for the all-volunteer, donation-sponsored, nonprofit organization dedicated to saving abused, abandoned, and unwanted Miniature Schnauzers.

Good News for Pets
www.goodnewsforpets.com
Updated weekly, this site profiles people in the dog world, provides nutrition facts, and updates legal issues.

Pet World Radio
www.petworldradio.net
Steve Dale's guide to pet radio.

American Society for the Prevention of Cruelty to Animals
www.aspca.org
Features humane education and advocacy information, with a link to the ASPCA Poison Control Center.

American Veterinary Medical Association
www.avma.org
The latest veterinary medical news.

Karen Pryor Clickertraining

www.clickertraining.com

Here's everything you want to know about clicker training—products, books, training tips.

Dog Friendly

www.dogfriendly.com

Information about traveling with dogs, including guidebooks.

Canine Freestyle Federation

www.canine-freestyle.com

This site is devoted to canine freestyle—dancing with your dog. There's information about freestyle events, tips, and even music to choose!

Index

Photo Credits:

Courtesy of the American Kennel Club: 21, 22, 23, 25
Kent Dannen: 4–5, 11, 14, 19, 39, 62, 64, 79, 96, 104, 124
Jean M. Fogle: 12, 61, 93
Bonnie Nance Photography: 1, 8–9, 17, 20, 26, 27, 28, 29, 32, 33, 34, 38, 40–41, 42, 44, 45, 46, 49, 52, 53, 54, 55, 56, 58, 66, 69, 71, 72, 73, 80, 82, 86, 88, 89, 91, 97, 102–103, 125, 128, 130, 132, 133, 134